Forbid Not Prophecy

Tom Barkey

Power Living Ministries
Anaheim, California

Unless otherwise indicated, all scriptural quotations are from the *New King James Version* of the Bible.

Forbid Not Prophecy
ISBN 0-9626910-1-1
Copyright © 1991 by
Tom Barkey
1026 S. East Street
Anaheim, CA 92805
U.S.A.

Published by
Power Living Ministries
1026 S. East Street
Anaheim, CA 92805

Printed in the United States of America.
All rights reserved under International Copyright
Law. Contents and/or cover may not be reproduced in
whole or in part in any form without the express
written consent of the publisher.

Contents

Foreword

Introduction

Section 1: Office of Prophet 1

1. Forbid Not Prophecy 3
2. Warning About Prophecy 15
3. Old and New Testament Prophets 25
4. Four Categories of Prophets 47
5. Prophetic Gifting 55
6. Prophetic Ministry 61
7. Office of Prophet 63
8. Administering the Prophetic Office 67
9. Judging Prophecy 73

Section 2: Gift of Prophecy 79

10. Desire to Prophesy 81
11. Preparation to Prophesying 91
12. Guidelines for Prophecy and Tongues 103
13. Questions About Prophecy 117

Foreword

I was fascinated to read Tom Barkey's manuscript, *Forbid Not Prophecy*. He has such a fresh and stimulating approach to the subject of prophecy for our times.

In chapter five, Tom defines the prophetic ministry as a declaration of what the Holy Spirit is saying to the Church. He has a good way of clarifying, simplifying, and illuminating these biblical truths.

I was also impressed with his definitions of inspirational prophesying in contrast with other forms of prophecy.

In recommending this book, I'm aware of how controversial the whole subject has become. Some reject any manifestations of the Holy Spirit totally, others are confused as to the difference between the gift of prophecy (which all believers are capable of participating in) and the office of prophet, which is a special calling. This book clarifies the difference.

I was especially interested in Tom's teaching on the four-tiered order of the prophetic gifts: (1) *Foundational Prophecy*, (2) *Prophetic Gifting*, (3) *Prophetic Ministry*, and (4) the *Office of the Prophet*. As a teacher/pastor, our brother places practical limits and restrictions on the operations of the prophetic gifts. There are others who want to operate in spiritual gifts without sensitivity, responsibility, or accountability.

Tom Barkey's book has good insights into the subject of prophecy. I suggest you read this book with an open Bible, an open mind, and an open heart.

Dick Mills

Introduction

Revelation 19:20, "I fell at His feet to worship Him, but He said to me, 'See that you do not do that! I am your fellow servant, and of your brethren who have the testimony of Jesus. Worship God! For the testimony of Jesus is the spirit of prophecy.'"

This verse tells us that the "spirit of prophecy" is the testimony of Jesus.

When prophecy is operating correctly in the Church, it should testify to the ministry of Jesus Christ. Prophecy is not intended to confirm or recognize a particular person's ministry, church, or person. Prophecy should not exalt the man, but testify to Jesus.

As you read this book, you'll learn about the office of the prophet and the gift of prophecy. You'll learn how they can operate for the edification of the Church. It's extremely important that our desire to prophesy should be one that the Church be edified, not that we, as individuals, may be recognized.

I Thessalonians 5:15-22 says, "See that no one renders evil for evil to anyone, but always pursue that which is good both for yourselves and for all. Rejoice always, pray without ceasing, in everything give thanks; for this is the will of God in Christ Jesus for you. Do not quench the Spirit. Do not despise prophecies. Test all things; hold fast to what is good. Abstain from every form of evil."

In these verses, Paul writes instructions that we are not to render evil to anyone, but pursue what is good, both for ourselves and for others. In our pursuit for spiritual maturity, we should remember that God wants to edify the Body of Christ.

God has given a gift — prophecy — as one vehicle that will bring edification to the Body of Christ. We're not supposed to despise prophecy but, literally, encourage it. As we encourage prophecy, let us encourage the edification of the Church.

Remember the words of the Apostle John in his writing of the Book of Revelation, ". . . the testimony of Jesus is the spirit of prophecy."

This book will help you develop in the gift of prophecy, and if you are called to the office of prophet, it will help you recognize where you are today and where God will be taking you in the future.

Tom Barkey

Section 1
Office of Prophet

Chapter 1
Forbid Not Prophecy

"Are there prophets today?"

"Is there prophecy in the Church today?"

Paul answered these questions in I Corinthians 12:28- 31:

And God has appointed these in the church: first apostles, second prophets, third teachers, after that miracles, then gifts of healings, helps, administrations, varieties of tongues.

Are all apostles? Are all prophets? Are all teachers? Are all workers of miracles?

Do all have gifts of healings? Do all speak with tongues? Do all interpret?

But earnestly desire the best gifts. And yet I show you a more excellent way.

So we see from Paul's list of gifts in the Church (verse 28) that God *has* appointed that there be prophets in the Church today.

The Church and the Gifts Are Alive!

Is the *Church* still here today? Then these gifts or offices are still here today, because they have been placed in the *Church*. As long as the *Church* is present, these offices will be present.

As long as there is a *Church*, there are apostles. As long as there is a *Church*, there are prophets. As long as there is a

Church, there are teachers. Paul goes on to list gifts of healings, helps, and administrations.

If the *Church* hasn't left, neither have these offices or gifts!

Prophets in the Church

We find another important reference to prophets in I Corinthians 14:29:

Let two or three prophets speak, and let the others judge.

This verse states that there should be at least two or three prophets present and operating in each church. Why else would Paul limit the number of prophets speaking to two or three in a public service?

Paul is telling the Church at Corinth what limitations are on the *office of prophet*, or the speaking of prophecy. Therefore, if there are not supposed to be prophets, or if there is not supposed to be prophecy, why is Paul telling us to limit it?

Look at verse 37:

If anyone thinks himself to be a prophet or spiritual, let him acknowledge that the things which I write to you are the commandments of the Lord.

Paul is saying, "If you think you are a prophet, you need to acknowledge that what I am saying is a commandment from God." In other words, "Yes, there are prophets!"

However, many people today teach that the *office of prophet* has passed away, and there are no more prophets in the land. But the Bible declares that there *are* prophets today — literally in every church that will allow this gift from the Holy Spirit to operate.

The Old Testament Prophet

For further light on this subject, we need to consider the role the Old Testament prophets held in their society. In the Old Testament, three offices were anointed by the Holy Spirit to do what God had called them to do:

1. King of Israel
2. Prophets
3. Priests

Some people teach that the Old Testament prophets are equivalent to the New Testament prophets. Others teach that the Old Testament prophet is equivalent to the New Testament apostle.

The Old Testament *prophet* does not exist in the Church. The Old Testament *priest* does not exist in the Church. Nor does the Old Testament *king* exist in the Church.

For the Church is the mystery that was hidden in the Old Testament. It is revealed in the New Testament, and it is exposed, or manifested, by Jesus Christ today.

Thus, the Old Testament prophet cannot be compared with the New Testament prophet, and vice versa. You cannot look at an Old Testament prophet to find out how a New Testament prophet should operate, because *they are not even the same office!*

Ephesians 4:7-11 says of Jesus:

But to each one of us grace was given according to the measure of Christ's gift.

Therefore He says: "When He ascended on high, He led captivity captive, and gave gifts to men."

(Now this, "He ascended" — what does it mean but that He also first descended into the lower parts of the earth?

He who descended is also the One who ascended far above all the heavens, that He might fill all things.)

And He Himself gave some to be apostles, some prophets, some evangelists, and some pastors and teachers.

Prophet, Priest, and King in the Church Age

Jesus is the "He" referred to in verse 11. It says Jesus Himself "gave some to be *apostles.*" Are there apostles in the Old Testament? No! It says Jesus Himself gave "some *prophets,* some *evangelists,* and some *pastors* and *teachers.*" Are there evangelists in the Old Testament? No! Are there pastors and teachers in the Old Testament? No! But there are prophets.

These ministry gifts were a mystery in the Old Testament. They were non-operational then; they are manifested in the New Testament through the giving of gifts by Jesus Christ.

As we saw, in the Old Testament, there were only three groups of people anointed by the Holy Spirit:

1. King of Israel
2. Prophets
3. Priests

But in the New Testament, *every believer* is anointed by the Holy Spirit. Thus, the prophet, priest, and king of the Old Testament is the "saint" of the New Testament.

You are a prophet, priest, and king! The Bible says "that all may prophesy." Not all believers are *prophets*, but all may *prophesy*.

The Prophets Jesus Gave

Those who try to find out how a New Testament prophet should act, talk, or prophesy by looking at Old Testament examples are making a grave mistake, because they are not the same office at all.

According to Mark 16:16-18, all of us believers have been commissioned to preach the Gospel, go into all the world, lay hands on the sick, and speak in new tongues.

Under the Old Testament, the prophet was the one who proclaimed the Word of the Lord and the coming of the Messiah (the first and second coming of Jesus).

Jesus has come for the first time, has been resurrected, has given gifts to the Church, and has given the Church to the world. Now the Church is to fulfill its priestly ministry to the whole world by bringing people to Jesus Christ, for we have been given the ministry of reconciliation.

Differences Between Prophets

Let us look at some differences between Old and New Testament prophets. First, under the Old Testament, the prophet received divine revelation from the Holy Spirit. In the New Testament, prophecy, according to Romans 12:6, is given *according to our faith.*

Let us first examine Romans 12:1 and 2:

I beseech you therefore, brethren, by the mercies of God, that you present your bodies a living sacrifice, holy, acceptable to God, which is your reasonable service.

And do not be conformed to this world, but be transformed by the renewing of your mind, that you may prove what is that good and acceptable and perfect will of God.

It says you should present your body a living sacrifice to God and do His perfect will. The words "reasonable service" literally should be translated "spiritual worship." Your spiritual worship is living for God!

Your mind is to be renewed on a daily basis, which will cause you to be changed into God's perfect will. When you hear the Word of God and you apply it to your life, you are changing your life into God's perfect will.

From this we see we have a responsibility to nurture our lives and the gifts that God has given us, and to find God's good and acceptable and perfect will for our life.

Verse 3:

For I say, through the grace given to me, to everyone who is among you, not to think of himself more highly than he ought to think, but to think soberly, as God has dealt to each one a measure of faith.

This means you are not to be something that you are not supposed to be in the Body of Christ. You are not supposed to live something that you have not been called to live. You are supposed to live by faith.

Ask for what you believe God has told you to do, and do it by faith.

Prophesy by Faith

Then it says in verses 4-6:

For as we have many members in one body, but all the members do not have the same function,

so we, being many, are one body in Christ, and individually members of one another.

Having then gifts differing according to the grace that is given to us, let us use them: if prophecy, *let us prophesy in proportion to our faith.*

New Testament prophets prophesy *according to their faith*. Under the Old Testament, the prophets prophesied *according to divine revelation*. They either had a dream or a vision, or the audible voice of God gave them a divine word and they spoke it.

Second, under the Old Testament, if you were wrong in your prophecy, you were stoned. The New Testament tells us to merely judge prophecy. (Thankfully.)

The third difference between the Old and the New Testament prophet is that there were few prophets living on the earth at any one time in Old Testament days. At one time there was a school of the prophets, but usually there weren't many prophets.

In the New Testament, we see that there can be a minimum of three prophets in each church. That's a big difference. It illustrates that the Old Testament prophet has little in common with the New Testament prophet.

A Different Office of Prophet

The fourth difference between the prophets is that the Old Testament prophets had authority over national leaders, whereas New Testament prophets have been given authority in the local church (but not over the pastor, as you'll see). Today we live under different governmental structures than they did in the Old Testament.

The Old Testament tells of prophets being sent to the king. Yes, we have prophets today going to kings and presidents, but they don't have authority over them. They are sent there as messengers.

Today we have a new priesthood. We have a new kingship. We have a new authority. We have a new relationship. We are in a new covenant with new offices.

Unfortunately, there are some Christians who look at such Old Testament prophets as Elijah, Elisha, Joel, and Moses and think that if you're really a prophet, you'll act just like they did.

No, we have a different *office of prophet* today, just like the apostle is new, the pastor is new, the teacher is new, the evangelist is new, and the gifts of healing through the Body of Christ are new.

To me, the first chapter of Hebrews is the second most powerful Scripture in the New Testament that proves that the Old Testament prophet is not operating in the Church today. Let's look at Hebrews 1:1:

God, who at various times and in different ways spoke in time past to the fathers by the prophets . . . .

That's clear enough, isn't it? God spoke in times past — meaning before Jesus' birth, death, and resurrection — to the fathers by the prophets. Thus, God's vehicle of speaking to His people in the Old Testament was through the office of the prophet. This was just clarified in verse 1. Verse 2 continues:

has in these last days spoken to us by His Son, whom He has appointed heir of all things, through whom He also made the worlds.

The New Testament Prophet, Priest, and King

So verses 1 and 2 clearly state that God has shifted from speaking through the *office of prophet* to speaking through Jesus to believers. And Jesus says, "All authority in heaven and earth has been given unto me; therefore you go." Jesus has commissioned *us* as *prophet, priest, and king* into this world! He says, "You go."

He says, "I have given you gifts." He has released new gifts into the Church. He has given us the gift of the apostle, the prophet, the evangelist, and the pastor/teacher.

In old times, before the resurrection of Jesus Christ, God spoke through His prophets to our fathers. He has, in these last days, spoken to us by His Son. That's a clear-cut change of how He is going to minister to the Body of Christ.

Scriptural Proof

Now turn to Luke 7. This Scripture is so important. I believe it is the first Scripture that declares that the *office of prophet* in the Old Testament is clearly different from the New Testament prophet. Luke 7:24-26 says:

> **When the messengers of John had departed, He began to speak to the multitudes concerning John: "What did you go out into the wilderness to see? A reed shaken by the wind?**
>
> **"But what did you go out to see? A man clothed in soft garments? Indeed those who are gorgeously appareled and live in luxury are in kings' courts.**
>
> **"But what did you go out to see? A prophet? Yes, I say to you, and more than a prophet."**

Jesus clearly defines John the Baptist as a prophet. There is no question about that, according to His comments in verse 27:

> **"This is he of whom it is written: 'Behold, I send My messenger before Your face, who will prepare Your way before You.'**

Which messenger was that? In what spirit did John come? The spirit of Elijah. Jesus continues in verse 28:

> **"For I say to you, among those born of women there is not a greater prophet than John the Baptist...."**

Jesus says right here that the greatest prophet who has ever lived was John the Baptist! If Jesus, the Son of God, declares that John the Baptist was the greatest prophet who has ever lived, are you going to argue with that?

We don't know of one miracle performed by John the Baptist, yet Jesus still called him the greatest prophet who ever lived! What did John do during his ministry? He preached. He simply preached repentance and the coming of the Messiah. He prepared the way of the Lord; he prepared the way for His first coming.

Now let's look at the remainder of verse 28:

... but he who is least in the kingdom of God is greater than he."

Here, Jesus is saying that the *least* person in the Church is greater than the *greatest* prophet of the Old Testament! Notice from this verse that *the Old Testament prophet is not equivalent to the New Testament prophet, because the least saint in the New Testament is greater than the greatest prophet in the Old Testament.*

Greater in Proclamation

This does not mean that the modern believer is greater in the sense of a *prophetic ministry*, but greater in the sense of proclaiming the Word of the Lord. Yes, the Old Testament prophet was anointed — but so are you! You are anointed by the Holy Spirit. You are declared to be a king and a priest in this world. You have been commissioned to preach the Gospel. And you have been sent to prepare the world for the Second Coming of Jesus Christ. So we are here declaring the Word of the Lord in the world.

New Testament Prophets

Therefore, we are now required to go to the New Testament and look at examples of New Testament prophets to understand how they minister and what they do. Then we can follow that ministry. The Bible clearly states that there are prophets today, but as we have seen, they are not equal to the Old Testament prophets.

For example, the Old Testament prophets proclaimed that the Messiah was about to come. Jesus came, and He is manifested. Did you know that Jesus was an Old Testament prophet? Then He died, was resurrected, and became a New Testament prophet.

Jesus is the only One who was both. The Bible also declares Him to be an apostle, a deacon, a shepherd, and a pastor. Jesus encompasses every ministering office there is. We are simply extensions of Jesus.

We will see this in detail in the following Scriptures:

> And God has appointed these in the church: first apostles, second prophets, third teachers, after that miracles, then gifts of healings, helps, administrations, varieties of tongues.
>
> I Corinthians 12:28

God says these are in the Church today. Now look at Ephesians 4:11:

> And He Himself [this is Jesus] gave some to be apostles, some prophets, some evangelists, and some pastors and teachers.

Jesus Speaks To Us Today

Hebrews 1:2 says:

> ... in these last days [God has] spoken to us by His Son....

Have you ever gone to a church and found Jesus standing on the platform or behind the pulpit preaching to you? But God says in these last days He will be speaking to us by His Son.

Jesus is an apostle, a prophet, a pastor, an evangelist, a teacher, a deacon, and an elder. How is He speaking to the Church today? He is speaking through His gifts that He has given.

I believe the New Testament apostles, prophets, evangelists, pastors, and teachers are mysteries that were hidden from the Old Testament, to be revealed in the Church Age. And I believe further that they are to walk in a greater anointing than the Old Testament prophets did. I believe they are to be greater than the greatest of the Old Testament prophets. I believe they are to walk in a more powerful presence of God than the Old Testament prophets.

New Testament Mysteries

> Now to Him who is able to establish you according to my gospel and the preaching of Jesus Christ, according to the revelation of the mystery which was kept secret since the world began

> **but now has been made manifest, and by the prophetic Scriptures has been made known to all nations, according to the commandment of the everlasting God, for obedience to the faith....**
>
> **Romans 16:25,26**

I believe that the offices Jesus placed in the Church were "mysteries," according to this Scripture. They have now been revealed through the prophetic Scriptures, so we can go back to the Old Testament and see the Messianic prophecies fulfilled and also see His offices working today in the land.

So in Romans 16:25 and 26 we find that Jesus has been manifesting the mystery. Paul says, "I preach a mystery." The New Testament is full of mysteries, meaning that God is revealing things to us that most of the Old Testament saints never knew or participated in.

Knowing God

The Old Testament saints had one family or tribe of priests, the Levites. In the New Testament, everyone who calls on the Name of the Lord is a priest.

Different kinds of prophetic offices are described in the Bible. We see *Old Testament prophets* and *seers* (those who have visions). There are *New Testament prophets*, and there are *false prophets*, both Old and New Testament. *Tribulation prophets* are found in the Book of Revelation. (There are even prophets in the Tribulation who are neither in the Church nor in the Old Testament!)

Who are we in the Body of Christ? I John 4:7 answers this question:

> **Beloved, let us love one another, for love is of God; and everyone who loves is born of God and knows God.**

This means that when you call on the Name of the Lord Jesus Christ, not only are you born of God, but you enter into a relationship with God, and you begin to know God.

During Old Testament times, people went to the Temple to find God. They went to Mt. Sinai to see God. They went to Moses and the priests to have them intercede between them and God.

But in the New Testament, the Bible says that you can come *boldly* to the throne of grace to receive God's help, mercy, and blessing in your time of need!

Look at Revelation 1:4b-6:

> **. . . Grace to you and peace from Him who is and who was and who is to come, and from the seven Spirits who are before His throne,**
>
> **and from Jesus Christ, the faithful witness, the firstborn from the dead, and the ruler over the kings of the earth. To Him who loved us and washed us from our sins in His own blood,**
>
> **and has made us kings and priests to His God and Father, to Him be glory and dominion forever and forever. Amen.**

Revelation 1:6 says that you are a king and a priest. I Corinthians 14 says that all may prophesy. The office of king, priest, and prophet of the Old Testament is manifested in the New Testament saint. We are the fulfillment of the Old Testament law!

We have been made righteous through the grace of God. We have been delivered from the power of darkness and translated into the kingdom of the Son of His love.

- We are now ministering one to another in a prophetic way.

- We are now ministering to God the Father in a priestly way.

- We are now ministering to this world in a kingly way.

- God has called us now to be prophets, priests, and kings, that we should declare the Word of the Lord in the world.

Chapter 2

Warnings About Prophecy

I want to share a word of caution about prophecy. In particular, believers should be extremely cautious about personal prophecy.

What is personal prophecy? I define it as one person going to another and saying, "God has told me this and this about you."

I believe personal prophecy should come from the gifts in those whom God has set in the Church. These would be gifts that have been judged prophetically, have matured prophetically, and have been proven over a period of time to be accurate.

This means, *I believe that the majority of personal prophecies delivered to believers should come from the pulpit ministries;* from those whom God has set in the Church to edify and build up believers.

The second way I have observed that God will use personal prophecy is through someone others already have respect for in areas of their spiritual maturity, accuracy, and edification. That person has been known to have been used for personal prophecy in the past and they have a good track record.

Warnings From Scripture

Unfortunately, people can get in the way of God's blessings by trying to prove themselves as "spiritual." As Paul warns us in I Corinthians 14:37:

If anyone thinks himself to be a prophet or spiritual, let him acknowledge that the things which I write to you are the commandments of the Lord.

In other words, Paul is saying, "If people who say they are prophets will not allow themselves to be judged according to the Word, then forget about their words! If they will not make the following statement, walk away! "Fine, take the word that God has given to me and see what you think — judge it according to the Bible, judge it according to your experiences with the Holy Spirit, and if it's not accurate, let's forget it."

James issues a similar warning:

But if you have bitter envy and self-seeking in your hearts, do not boast and lie against the truth.

This wisdom does not descend from above, but is earthly, sensual, demonic.

For where envy and self-seeking exist, confusion and every evil thing will be there.

But the wisdom that is from above is first pure, then peaceable, gentle, willing to yield, full of mercy and good fruits, without partiality and without hypocrisy.

James 3:14-17

What this says to me about *prophetic ministry* is that if you are jealous over someone else's anointing, you will fall into an evil wisdom. You will use your gift to try to control other people's lives. You will be overly eager to prove yourself to be spiritual, and you will end up hurting people. So you need to be cautious and move slowly when it comes to prophecy and prophetic offices.

Automatic Error

I believe that God is manifesting the *office of prophet* in a greater way during the decade of the '90s. However, some words of caution are necessary here.

If we start to look to the prophets' spiritual gifts and judge the prophets to be morally correct in their lifestyle *simply because of the spiritual gifts* working in them, we are automatically in error!

You cannot look at prophets who have miracles, healings, and accurate words taking place in their ministry and say they're *perfect* — because they're not. Remember, God works through people who will yield themselves to Him.

Required: A Walk of Holiness

In today's world, God is asking all of us to walk in holiness in order for the Church to be pure and godly. A walk of holiness means a walk of faith. It is a walk of separation from the world; of declaring and doing what God wants us to do.

First, God wants us to be pure in heart. That is, He does not want us to be hypocrites. In the Book of Luke, Jesus declared that we should not be as the scribes and Pharisees, who were hypocrites. They said one thing, but inside they were something else.

Jesus said that what is inside them will be declared on the housetops. When these prophetic offices mature and develop, some things are going to be declared on the housetops! Those who are living a hypocritical lifestyle should beware, because *hypocrites will be exposed.*

God is warning us now to clean up our lives, live in the Word, be spiritual believers, and walk in the Spirit, not in the flesh.

Judgment Begins in the Pulpit

God is going to expose the secrets of men's hearts, and He will begin with the hypocrites. He has already begun in the pulpit, which is scriptural. Peter says that judgment begins in the house of God (I Peter 4:17).

Several years ago, there were men who stood in the pulpit and said one thing, and then went behind closed doors and did something else. God says that is hypocrisy, and it will be declared on the housetops. How much more exposed can you get than be on TV? God declared through television the sins of those people who had lived hypocritical lifestyles.

Prophecy for Personal Gain

Another aspect of prophecy to be cautious about is people who use prophecy for their own advantage.

I was once an associate pastor of a church, and I saw the pastor use prophecy for his own personal gain. When I saw it, I said, "I'm not going to participate in this!" I resigned and left the next week.

This is what happened. A certain man had become somewhat unhappy with the way some things were taking place in the church. He had made an appointment with the pastor, and they saw each other during the Sunday School hour before the church service.

The man had come to the pastor for help. The man was just sharing his feelings about the church and the difficulties he was going through.

The pastor sat there politely, agreeing with the man. To an onlooker, it seemed to be a wonderful meeting. The pastor seemed to be so understanding. The man got up, no doubt thinking, "We're going to get some things straightened out now."

Because of my position in the church, I knew what the meeting had been about. We went into the service. The pastor got up and started to preach. For the next hour I listened to him chew that man out. *And he did it through so-called prophecy!* He walked up to the man and gave him a "word from God," just raking him over the coals. He even ended his rebuke with "Thus saith the Lord"!

No one else knew what was going on, but I knew. The man just sat there, getting beet red, sinking into his seat. He never returned to the church again, and I don't blame him.

Guidelines for Prophecy

This was a horrible example where a man used "prophecy" to correct someone else. You need to know that there are people like this pastor who will use so-called

Warnings About Prophecy

prophecy to their own advantage — and it will destroy people. Prophecies must be subjected to the following guidelines:

- Judged according to the Word of God.
- Delivered in the spirit of humility.
- Delivered in the spirit of edification.
- Delivered in the spirit of comfort.
- Clearly intended to help people.

Before that happened, I'd had a similar experience with that particular pastor. I preached a sermon on Easter night and I thought he had agreed with the topic, but evidently, he hadn't!

For the next three weeks, I didn't get to preach as I was supposed to on Sunday nights. And I didn't know what was going on.

Four weeks later, on a Sunday night, the pastor preached the same message I had preached, but correcting me. He had never come to me privately and told me that perhaps I was in error, that he disagreed with my doctrine, or anything like that. He just preached his version of the message and ended it with, "Thus saith the Lord."

He came to me after the service and said, "There. Now do you understand?"

People like him are speaking false prophecies to get more money in offerings. People like him are making so-called prophecies to make people feel so sorry for them or guilty that they will give them money, cars, clothing, and other things.

My friends, situations like this are dangerous; especially in the decade of the '90s, because this is a decade of power, prophecy, and prayer.

There are prophets in the Church today. Whenever there's something *true*, there's something *false*. That means there are going to be false prophets, too.

Obedient Servants

God wants us, the Church, to develop into obedient servants through those whom the Holy Spirit can give profound words of encouragement to others. Such servants, however, must also be deeply humble before the Lord in order to be effective. God will exalt the humble — but He will walk away from the proud!

For example, some people become lifted up after they give words from the Lord that help people. They get into pride. Their attitude is, "That was a good word, wasn't it? Want to hear some more? I'm God's gift to the prophetic office!" Simply stated, these people are going to have problems.

Foundational Prophecy

According to I Corinthians 14:3, *foundational prophecy* should do three things:

But he who prophesies speaks *edification* and *exhortation* and *comfort* to men.

Literally, it means to speak to the Church. The word "edification" here means to build up, to build *you* up, to help you, to strengthen you.

My friend, if prophecy comes out of a church congregation and *tears you down*, it's neither proper nor correct! *Corrective words from the Lord will not, and should not, come from the congregation.*

Why? Because it causes a division of authority. People respect the office of the pastor and the offices represented by the guest speakers he invites. The pastor has the ability to correct because the members of his church come to *him* for spiritual guidance.

As we have seen, a *foundational prophecy* should bring:

1. edification
2. exhortation
3. comfort

Easy To Understand

Now let's look at I Corinthians 14:8,9:

> For if the trumpet makes an uncertain sound, who will prepare himself for battle?
>
> So likewise you, unless you utter by the tongue words easy to understand, how will it be known what is spoken? For you will be speaking into the air.

Verses 8 and 9 say *prophecy should be easy to understand,* not mystical, or so allegorical that you can't make out what the person is saying. In other words, the speakers shouldn't be so heavenly minded that they're no earthly good.

The prophetic words they speak should help you, build you up, comfort you, encourage you, edify you, and continue to point you in the right spiritual direction.

Sometimes what happens is that God gives someone a word during their own prayer time. Then, when they get to church, they feel the anointing of God, and recall the Bible says that "all may prophesy." They think, "It's my turn now!" so they speak out some "revelation" learned alone with God.

They may say something strange, like, "God said, 'Miss the train, and you will be on your way to heaven.'" The rest of the congregation thinks, "What did he mean by *that?"* It meant something to the person who said it. (Maybe they worked for Amtrak!) God gave the person a word in their prayer time, and they got so excited, they shared out of their own revelation. What was said was not prophecy.

To sum up: *Foundational prophecy* should be easily understood. It should be edifying, exhorting, and comforting.

The Prophetic Office

The prophetic office is different from *foundational prophecy,* because everyone who prophesies is not necessarily a prophet. This means, all who give *foundational prophecies* do not stand in the *office of prophet.*

The prophetic office should be able to *give direction and correction* to you by giving you a choice. When saying something about your future, prophecy always gives you a choice; it doesn't leave you in the dark. God gives a word to you for a reason.

Another characteristic of this office is that it *establishes doctrines*, along with the other offices, as seen in Ephesians 4:11,12

> **And He Himself gave some to be apostles, some prophets, some evangelists, and some pastors and teachers,**
>
> **for the equipping of the saints for the work of ministry, for the edifying of the body of Christ.**

Old Testament Prophets

Prophets of the Old Testament were free-lance preachers called by God to proclaim His Word. They were not submissive to anyone except God.

Prophets of the New Testament are to be submissive to one another and to their pastor, as well as to the structure of church government in the church they are attending. This is a further difference between Old and New Testament prophets.

We hear more about prophets from Peter's sermon in Acts 3:

> **... whom heaven must receive until the times of restoration of all things, which God has spoken by the mouth of all His holy prophets since the world began.**
>
> **For Moses truly said to the fathers, "The Lord your God will raise up for you a Prophet like me from your brethren. Him you shall hear in all things, whatsoever He says to you.**
>
> **"And it shall come to pass that every soul who will not hear that Prophet shall be utterly destroyed from among the people."**
>
> **Yes, and all the prophets, from Samuel and those who follow, as many as have spoken, have also foretold these days.**

Warnings About Prophecy

You are sons of the prophets, and of the covenant which God made with our fathers, saying to Abraham, "And in your seed all the families of the earth shall be blessed."

To you first, God, having raised up His Servant Jesus, sent Him to bless you, in turning away every one of you from your iniquities.

Acts 3:21-26

The Old Testament prophets prophesied about Jesus. Jesus is now the New Testament prophet who has turned you away from your iniquities and has made you a servant of the living God.

Prophets and Apostles

New Testament prophets are subject to the Church, subject to one another, subject to their pastor, and subject to Church government. But they are also here to bring us into the fullness of Christ, along with the pastor and the apostle, as we saw in Ephesians 4.

In the next few years, we will continue to hear a great deal of teaching on *prophets*. And in the next seven years, we will start hearing some teaching about *apostles*.

However, just because you hear preaching about prophets doesn't mean that they hold the most important office in the Church. In fact, the New Testament mentions very little about them, and almost nothing about evangelists. It says the most about pastors and apostles, in that order.

All this interest in prophets and prophecy will cause some believers to depend on prophets to tell them what to do in their life. But the Bible says that is not their office. That is not what they are called to do. They are not called to lead you. The Holy Spirit is to lead you. You are not to become dependent upon a person.

A true prophet will always direct you to Jesus Christ, because He is the Prophet of the Church.

If a prophet walks into a pulpit and starts giving personal words, and signs and wonders start to happen, all the congregation will flock at his feet. The congregation should recognize, however, that he is not the only prophet in the Church, for the Head Prophet of the Church is Jesus Christ. Prophets today are to be subject and submissive to Him and to the government He has set in the Church.

True and False Prophets

I believe we are going to see *true prophets* raised up in our land. I believe there are true prophets already walking in the earth. In fact, there have been true prophets on earth as long as the Church has been here!

On the other hand, I also believe there will be more *false prophets* who will rise up. These will be people who will declare themselves to be prophets. Jesus warned us about these self-proclaimed prophets in Matthew 7:15:

Beware of false prophets, who come to you in sheep's clothing, but inwardly they are ravenous wolves.

Some of the false prophets will be caught up in the recognition and limelight, and will try to draw people to themselves. As we have seen, a true prophet will always lead people to Jesus Christ, to fellowship with other saints, and to the church.

I believe that people will flock to prophets, crying, "Give me a word! Give me a word!" This can be a temptation to the prophet to abuse the office God has given him by trying to control people's lives.

Therefore, we need to walk cautiously and prayerfully in these days, considering what the Holy Spirit wants in our lives. Realize that God wants us to be prophets, priests, and kings, and He wants to raise the *office of prophet* out of the church to minister to the church and help the church.

Make sure you judge everything by the Word of God and do God's Word. Don't flock to a man; flock to Jesus.

In the beginning, prophecy seminars will be held so we can receive instruction and know what God is going to do and how He is going to do it. But what should happen afterwards is that the prophets will be in the churches, prophesying two or three at a time.

Chapter 3
Old and New Testament Prophets

It is extremely important in order to have the correct understanding of Old and New Testament prophets that we understand Hebrews 1:1,2:

God, who at various times and in different ways spoke in time past to the fathers by the prophets,

has in these last days spoken to us by His Son, whom He has appointed heir of all things, through whom also He made the worlds.

The phrase "in time past" refers to the time *before* Jesus Christ came to the earth, died, and was resurrected. *Before* Jesus came, God spoke to His people by His prophets. They were His mouthpiece. Their duty was to tell the people what God wanted.

In the *Old Testament*, God spoke to all His people by the prophets. In the *New Testament*, however, He speaks by Jesus Christ!

Jesus, in His wisdom, gives gifts to the Church, as we found in Ephesians 4:11. These gifts can also be called "offices," and there are people who walk in particular offices. So whether you call it an office or a gift, it's fine; they still all come from Jesus Christ.

Mouthpieces for God

God's mouthpieces to the Church today are:
1. The Holy Spirit
2. The gifts (or offices) that are in the Church

First, the Holy Spirit will lead you into truth. Remember, the Book of I John says you have no need that anyone teach you, for you have an unction from the Holy One.

> **But the anointing which you have received from Him abides in you, and you do not need that anyone teach you; but as the same anointing teaches you concerning all things, and is true, and is not a lie, and just as it has taught you, you will abide in Him.**
>
> **I John 2:27**

This reference to the Holy Spirit indicates that the Holy Spirit is the Teacher, the Guide, the One who leads you into all truth.

The gifts or offices are the *apostle*, the *prophet*, the *evangelist*, the *pastor/teacher*. They are the mouthpieces for God in the earth. They declare what God wants to accomplish.

Therefore, these offices or gifts are the ones who should establish *doctrine*. They should give *direction*. They should give *correction*. They should give *guidance*.

They are the ones whom God has raised up. They work within His framework of organization so all things can be done decently and in order, because this is a commandment from God:

> **Let all things be done decently and in order.**
>
> **I Corinthians 14:40**

So we understand from Hebrews 1:1 that *today the Father speaks through the Son, and the Son speaks through His gifts.*

A Greater Prophet Than John

Keep this thought in mind when you read Jesus' statement in Luke 7:28:

> "For I say to you, among those born of women there is not a greater prophet than John the Baptist; but he who is least in the kingdom of God is greater than he."

Here Jesus declares that the *least* in the kingdom of heaven is *greater* than John the Baptist — yet John was the *greatest* prophet who ever lived!

That's quite a statement, isn't it? Jesus' reference to the kingdom was the Church that was to come after Him. It is here now, of course.

If the least in the kingdom is greater than John the Baptist, it means that prophets in the New Testament would be even greater than John was in their ability to speak on God's behalf!

The reason why John was so great is because he spoke the Word of God *exactly*. He spoke what God wanted to speak. He spoke on God's behalf.

If the least in the kingdom of heaven is greater than John the Baptist, how much greater are the prophet and the apostle in the New Testament?

The Greatest Prophets

John the Baptist was called the greatest prophet in the Old Testament because he declared God's will to the lost. He told them to repent. He did what God said to do. He was God's mouthpiece.

Today, every believer is God's mouthpiece to the lost world. Yes, there are gifts who are God's mouthpiece to the Body, but everyone in the Church is God's mouthpiece to the lost!

So instead of having a few prophets running around the land telling people to repent, God has His whole Body — the Body of Christ — telling the world. We are preserving the world and declaring its salvation. We have a big job, or commission — the commission of reconciliation — and we need to be doing our job.

Granted, there are people within the Church who have been given gifts that they might proclaim God's Word for the Church, and they need to move in a supernatural way.

I think it's time that pastors begin to step out and be supernatural pastors. I think it's time for prophets to step out and be supernatural prophets. I think it's time for apostles to come forth as God wills, and for things to start happening in the land in a supernatural way.

New Revelations About Prophets

I believe that God is presently releasing significant revelation knowledge about the office of the prophet. In the next decade, we will learn more and more about prophets; this is just the beginning of the revelation knowledge that God is going to release.

I believe God is releasing more revelation knowledge about the prophets because He is raising up more prophets than ever before.

Some people are trying to teach studies on apostles and apostleship, but I don't believe that information has even been released into revelation yet. I don't believe that the teachers are even able to find the depth and the fullness of an *apostle*, because God's focus is on *prophets* right now!

As we grow step by step, God says, "Now I'm going to release this further wisdom." He releases wisdom slowly, according to His timetable, so we won't be overwhelmed by it in our maturing process.

New Testament Offices Today

There are people who say that the Old Testament *prophet* is today's *apostle*. I don't believe the Bible says that at all.

I believe the prophet, priest, and king of the Old Testament is the saint today, because of Jesus' statement that the least in the kingdom of heaven is greater than the greatest prophet of the Old Testament. That makes a major difference in the relationship of offices, doesn't it?

The apostle, prophet, evangelist, pastor/teacher in the world today are *new* offices ordained by Jesus Christ on the Day of Pentecost. These offices are *in* the Church — not *before* the Church, and not *after* the Church.

Let's turn to Peter's teaching in Acts 10:34,35:

Then Peter opened his mouth and said: "In truth I perceive that God shows no partiality.

"But in every nation whoever fears Him and works righteousness is accepted by Him."

Who is Peter sent to? He is an apostle to the Jews. That means, this is *an apostle* speaking!

Prophets' Limitations

There are people who say that prophets can speak exact words from God; that prophets are one hundred percent accurate — the way Catholics believe that everything the Pope says is infallible.

I'm sorry, but everything the Pope says is not infallible, and everything the prophet says in the latter days is not infallible. He or she can make an utterance that is completely from the heart of God, and one hundred percent the word of God, but *not every word a prophet speaks is the word of God*.

Why? Because every prophet is going to be tinted by his doctrine; he's going to be influenced by what he believes. He will prophesy limited to his doctrine. That's why the Bible says we should judge every prophecy according to the Bible.

Here is Peter, an apostle, who states, "In truth, I *perceive*...." He did not say, "The Holy Spirit has shown me," "God has declared," or "I know absolutely."

God wants you to grow in maturity and common-sense. If we start to look to prophets and exalt them, we will eventually be disappointed, because we will eventually see their weaknesses. Then we will walk away discouraged.

Manipulative Prophets

There are prophets in the land who are declaring themselves to be the authoritative voice of God. They are saying, "You'd better heed me." They use scriptures like, "Touch not God's anointed" and "Obey the prophets" to get their way.

A prophet doesn't need to bully his way through the Body of Christ. Either he's true, or he isn't. Either he's a prophet, or he's not.

If you hear of a prophet who does not belong to (regularly attend) a local church, you might as well not listen to him or her. During the 1980s, God restored the pastor's ministry and the local church, and He has started to move in the local church. God is not going to leave that movement to go outside again and do something else.

Prophets' Place in Church Government

We have found through the local church that God wants Body ministry, where the Body is participating. Beware if someone walks away from the local church, sets himself in office, and says, "I'm a prophet. I don't go to church, I don't have a pastor. I just go and minister wherever God leads me. God leads me, and you're going to have to obey me! Pastors are supposed to submit to me."

I would advise you to walk away from such a person. Even if the man or the woman is teaching and preaching something that seems good, I would not link myself with that ministry, because it's going to collapse someday. Why? Because if you're not in harmony with the local church, you're not in harmony with what God is doing in the earth.

God is moving *in* the Church, and God has set prophets *in* the Church. The prophet is to be in the Church, not outside of the Church.

Yes, there are prophets who travel from church to church, but they need to be submitted to a local church.

More than any of the offices, a prophet needs to be judged. In fact, the Bible says if a prophet prophesies, let the other prophets judge him:

Let two or three prophets speak, and let the others judge.

I Corinthians 14:29

It seems to be within the makeup of prophets that they need to have someone over them, because it will help them stay in line with the move of the Church.

As soon as a prophet starts exalting himself above all the pastors and declares himself to be greater than anyone else, you might as well disregard them.

Pre-Ordained Experiences

Peter continues his message, starting with verse 35 of Acts 10:

"But in every nation whoever fears Him and works righteousness is accepted by Him.

"The word which God sent to the children of Israel, preaching peace through Jesus Christ — He is Lord of all —

"that word you know, which was proclaimed throughout all Judea, and began from Galilee after the baptism which John preached:

"how God anointed Jesus of Nazareth with the Holy Spirit and with power, who went about doing good and healing all who were oppressed by the devil, for God was with Him.

"And we are witnesses of all things which He did both in the land of the Jews and in Jerusalem, whom they killed by hanging on a tree.

"Him God raised up on the third day, and showed Him openly,

"not to all the people, but to witnesses chosen before by God, even to us who ate and drank with Him after He rose from the dead.

Acts 10:35-41

Peter is saying that the people Jesus appeared to were pre-ordained by God to have this experience.

Now let us look more closely at verses 40 through 42:

Him God raised up on the third day, and showed Him openly,

not to all the people, but to witnesses chosen before by God, even to us who ate and drank with Him after He rose from the dead.

And He commanded us to preach to the people, and to testify that it is He who was ordained by God to be Judge of the living and the dead.

After Jesus arose from the dead, He was eating with His disciples, and He said, "I am He that they prophesied about. Now do you believe it? Now will you go and tell other people?"

Continuing with verse 43:

To Him all the prophets witness that, through His name, whoever believes in Him will receive remission of sins.

This verse says all the Old Testament prophets were proclaiming to people who needed salvation that if they would call on the name of the Messiah, they would have remission of sins. That's what their prophecy was pointing to.

Today, prophets in the New Testament are not saying to the Church who are already born again, "You must be saved." Instead, they are building them up in their priesthood and sending them out to the world.

The Ministry of Reconciliation

We, the priests, are going to the world and telling them that they must be born again. This is *the ministry of reconciliation*.

This ministry was *not* given to the apostles, prophets, evangelists, pastors, or teachers. It was given to the saints! Believers in the Church are to go out and tell *other* people about Jesus Christ.

Romans 3:21:

But now the righteousness of God apart from the law is revealed, being witnessed by the Law and the Prophets.

The law of Moses and the prophets witnessed our manifestation. In other words, *we* are the manifestation of their prophecies!

Prophesying in Part

This doesn't mean that someone who stands in the pulpit, speaking on behalf of God, will say everything correctly. In fact, the Bible declares that we only know *in part*, and we only prophesy *in part*, so every preacher is only sharing the *part* he has.

You may argue, "Well, why should we even listen to any preacher?"

Because we live by faith, not by sight. Because the whole system that God has ordained in the Church is to be by faith. The just shall live by faith.

Peter touched on this subject when he preached:

that the genuineness of your faith, being much more precious than gold that perishes, though it is tested by fire, may be found to praise, honor, and glory at the revelation of Jesus Christ,

whom having not seen you love. Though now you do not see Him, yet believing, you rejoice with joy inexpressible and full of glory,

I Peter 1:7,8

Even though you don't see Jesus, you're still rejoicing that Jesus *is*, and that He has been raised from the dead.

The Changing of the Guard

Verses 9 through 11:

receiving the end of your faith — the salvation of your souls.

Of this salvation the prophets have inquired and searched diligently, who prophesied of the grace that would come to you,

searching what, or what manner of time, the Spirit of Christ who was in them was indicating when He testified beforehand the sufferings of Christ and the glories that would follow.

Look at verses 10 and 11. They state that the people who prophesied about our salvation had the spirit of Christ in them.

Look at verse 11. The phrase "searching what, or what manner of time, the Spirit of Christ who was in them" refers to the Old Testament prophets. The Spirit of Christ in them indicates that Christ testified beforehand about the sufferings He would experience and the glories that would follow.

What this is saying is, Jesus spoke in the Old Testament through the prophets. But in the New Testament, Jesus speaks through His gifts. Thus, there is a "changing of the guard," so to speak. God has moved from the Old Testament way of communication to the New Testament way.

The average person who was living for God in Old Testament times did not have the Holy Spirit living *inside* of him. The average person had to go to the Temple to visit God.

In the New Testament, it says *we* are the temple of the Holy Spirit. So we are the kings, the priests, and the prophets of the New Testament.

Eight New Testament Prophets

Eight prophets are named in the Book of Acts. Five of them are listed in Acts 13:1:

Now in the church that was at Antioch there were certain prophets and teachers: *Barnabas*, *Simeon* who was called Niger, *Lucius* of Cyrene, *Manaen* who had been brought up with Herod the tetrarch, and *Saul*.

Acts 15:32 lists *Judas* and *Silas* as prophets:

Now *Judas* and *Silas*, themselves being prophets also, exhorted the brethren with many words and strengthened them.

Then, in Acts 21:8 and 9 it says Phillip had four daughters who prophesied. It *doesn't* say they were *prophetesses*; it just says that they prophesied. So women do prophesy.

On the next day we ... entered the house of Phillip the evangelist, who was one of the seven, and stayed with him.

> Now this man had four virgin daughters who prophesied.

Finally, in Acts 21:10, Agabus is listed:

> And as we stayed many days, a certain prophet named *Agabus* came down from Judea.

The Foundation of the Church

In Luke 7:28, we saw that the least in the kingdom of God is greater than the greatest prophet in the Old Testament. This means that the New Testament prophets would be even greater than the Old Testament prophets. Even the apostles would be greater than they were!

Did you know that the Church was *founded* on the work of apostles and prophets? They are the ones who built the Church. They are the ones who established its foundation.

You may wonder why pastors were not used for the founding of the Church. You can't have a pastor until you have a congregation! And you can't have a congregation until you get people saved.

Supernatural Choices

Apostles were sent out to establish churches. Once congregations were formed, they were able to appoint pastors through the direction of the Holy Spirit. The pastors were able to lay hands on people and discern what gifts they were called to walk in. That is the supernatural way to get elders in the Church, isn't it?

Today, too many churches throughout the land *vote* for their favorite "personality," making them an elder. Consequently, there are many elders in churches who do not qualify to be elders, according to the standards set forth in I and II Timothy. (Popularity is not one of them.)

And then the church wonders why it has financial problems! It wonders why it has spiritual problems! The reason, of course, is because they have placed in their leadership men and women who aren't biblically qualified to be there.

Could we be so supernatural — so sensitive to the Holy Spirit — that we could lay hands on the people in the congregation and discern their gift, like Paul did with Timothy?

Paul laid hands on Timothy and realized what he was called to do. He didn't give Timothy the gift, but Paul was able to connect with his spirit and know that he was called to be — a pastor. Timothy did pastor, and Paul was able to nurture him and raise him up in that office.

Could we do that today? Yes, we can!

How many churches around this nation select deacons, elders, and board members because they like them, they look good, sound good, and they have a business? What about being *called* to leadership? What about being placed in leadership by the Holy Spirit?

I believe that churches that would place people in leadership by the Spirit would never have a church split! If those leaders work together in prayer and supplication, seeking God, the enemy could not get in and divide them.

God Adds Offices

As we studied, the Church was founded by apostles and prophets.

having been built on the foundation of the apostles and prophets, Jesus Christ Himself being the chief cornerstone,

in whom the whole building, being joined together, grows into a holy temple in the Lord,

in whom you also are being built together for a habitation of God in the Spirit.

Ephesians 2:20-22

This passage means that apostles and prophets were used to establish *doctrine, missions,* and *direction* at the beginning of the Church. They were God's mouthpiece for the beginning of the Church.

"Why aren't they still fulfilling this role, if this is what they should be doing?" you may ask.

The answer is, God has added to the apostles and prophets. He has added the offices of *evangelist,* and *pastor/teacher.*

> which in other ages was not made known to the sons of men, as it has now been revealed by the Spirit to His holy *apostles* and *prophets.*
>
> **Ephesians 3:5**

What this is saying is that God's plan and His will have been revealed to the offices that He placed in the Church. God is showing apostles, prophets, evangelists, and pastors/teachers His plan for the Church: *where* we are supposed to go and what is *the direction* we are supposed to take.

Prophets Should Warn

Look at II Peter 3. Did you know that prophets should be warning us of false teachers, false doctrine, and false prophets? Did you know that God has put prophets in the land to do that?

> **Beloved, I now write to you this second epistle (in both of which I stir up your pure minds by way of reminder),**
>
> **that you may be mindful of the words which were spoken before by the holy *prophets*, and of the commandment of us the *apostles* of the Lord and Savior.**
>
> **II Peter 3:1,2**

Peter states that there are apostles. Why did he do this? Remember, when these letters were being written, churches were just becoming established. Some had been in existence for only about ten years.

Churches were springing up everywhere, and the leaders at this time were the apostles and the prophets. As God's mouthpiece to the Church, they were giving instructions to the Church. They were declaring the will of God to the Church.

Peter Sees the Last Days

Let's look at what Peter says:

> knowing this first: that scoffers will come in the last days, walking according to their own lusts,
>
> and saying, "Where is the promise of His coming? For since the fathers fell asleep, all things continue as they were from the beginning of creation."
>
> II Peter 3:3,4

This means that people are going to show up declaring, "Hey, nothing's changed since the Old Testament. Nothing's changed since the old prophets. You keep saying, 'He's coming soon; He's coming soon.' *When* is He going to come? I don't think He'll come."

As Peter says, people will make fun of the *office of prophet* and of prophecy. There will be people who will also make fun of the doctrines that are established in the Church.

Peter continues:

> For this they willfully forget: that by the word of God the heavens were of old, and the earth standing out of water and in the water,
>
> by which the world that then existed perished, being flooded with water.
>
> But the heavens and the earth which now exist are kept in store by the same word, reserved for fire until the day of judgment and perdition of ungodly men.
>
> But, beloved, do not forget this one thing, that with the Lord one day is as a thousand years, and a thousand years as one day.
>
> The Lord is not slack concerning His promise, as some count slackness, but is longsuffering toward us, not willing that any should perish but that all should come to repentance.
>
> II Peter 3:5-9

Peter is declaring here that people are going to make fun of the doctrines of Christianity — the doctrines that prophets are bringing in — as well as prophecy and prophets themselves. They will say such things as, "You said you were healed, but I don't see it!"

Why God Delays

Peter is telling us, "Get ready — there's going to be more of this scoffing in the last days. Don't fret about God taking His time to fulfill what He has declared in your life."

Perhaps a godly person has given you a godly, edifying word, but that word has not yet come to pass. Have you ever said, *"When* is this ever going to happen?" It says here that God is not slack concerning His promises.

Do you want to know why certain things seem to take such a long time to happen? Do you want to know why God appears to be waiting?

Not Willing That Any Should Perish

According to verse 9, the whole reason God waits is because He's still working on people to get them *saved*.

The only reason your promise hasn't manifested as He promised, is because He is still working on individuals, waiting for some to repent and be born again.

God is holding things together so the greatest number of people may be saved. He is working all the promises in all the people so the most will come to know His Son, Jesus Christ.

Agabus Foretells

Let us be specific now and look at examples from the book of Acts of New Testament prophets, starting with Agabus.

> **And in these days prophets came from Jerusalem to Antioch.**
>
> **Then one of them, named Agabus, stood up and showed by the Spirit that there was going to be a great famine throughout all the world . . . .**
>
> **Acts 11:27, 28**

Agabus was a prophet who did not simply prophesy by word alone; he acted out his prophecies! We'll find later on that he took Paul's belt and went through a little skit with it.

So Agabus was a person who showed things that were to come. He was able to predict or foretell the future.

> ... there was going to be a great famine throughout all the world, which happened in the days of Claudius Caesar.
>
> Then the disciples, each according to his ability, determined to send relief to the brethren dwelling in Judea.
>
> This they also did, and sent it to the elders by the hands of Barnabas and Saul.
>
> Acts 11:28-30

This shows us that there was a certain prophet, in a group of prophets, who showed them there was going to be a famine in the whole world. When the famine took place, they were ready for it. They sent relief to the believers in Jerusalem.

So prophets have the ability to predict even what the weather is going to be, as the Holy Spirit tells them! I use the words "predict" and "foretell" as synonyms. I'm not using the world's definition of "prediction" as something outlandish that astrologists announce each January!

Ministering and Fasting

We have read about the people who are listed in Acts 13 as prophets. Now notice what these prophets do when they are together.

> As they ministered to the Lord and fasted, the Holy Spirit said, "Now separate to Me Barnabas and Saul for the work to which I have called them."
>
> Then, having fasted and prayed, and laid hands on them, they sent them away.
>
> Acts 13:2,3

Most theologians believe that Paul was a prophet *until* Acts 13, when this group of prophets was together, and one of them spoke out in the name of the Lord, and prophesied by the Holy Spirit that Paul and Barnabas were now apostles.

These prophets prophesied that these two were to change their office, from prophet to apostle.

In Acts 13, prophets are prophesying. *Prophets still prophesy today in the land!*

Studying Acts 13:6-11, we find that there were false prophets even in the New Testament.

Now when they had gone through the island to Paphos, they found a certain sorcerer, a false prophet, a Jew whose name was Bar-Jesus,

who was with the proconsul, Sergius Paulus, an intelligent man. This man called for Barnabas and Saul and sought to hear the word of God.

But Elymas the sorcerer (for so his name is translated) withstood them, seeking to turn the proconsul away from the faith.

Then Saul, who also is called Paul, filled with the Holy Spirit, looked intently at him

and said, "O full of all deceit and all fraud, you son of the devil, you enemy of all righteousness, will you not cease perverting the straight ways of the Lord?

"And now, indeed, the hand of the Lord is upon you . . . ."

Several verses earlier (verse 2), Paul was made an apostle. Now he shows up and points his finger at a false prophet. He says,

". . . you son of the devil, you enemy of all righteousness, will you not cease perverting the straight ways of the Lord?

"And now, indeed, the hand of the Lord is upon you, and you shall be blind, not seeing the sun for a time." And immediately a dark mist fell on him and he went around seeking someone to lead him by the hand.

Acts 13:10,11

Elymas was a false prophet who was trying to keep people away from the faith, to keep them from following Jesus, because of his own greed.

The Office of Apostle

Apostles, it appears, are the only office in the New Testament that turned someone over to Satan for the destruction of the flesh, spoke a word and someone died in their presence, or caused someone to be blind. We don't find examples where a pastor or a prophet did these things; only the apostles.

Therefore, I think that when we get more revelation on the office of the apostle, we will see that there was judgment in the house of God through their gift, and their hand was mighty.

You will recall that the Apostle Peter stood in front of a husband and wife, confronting them separately, and they fell dead at his feet. Now that's scary!

Imagine going to church and seeing someone die! The apostle walks over to a couple and says, "Have you done such and such?" If they lie to him, he says, "You have lied. These men have come to take you to your grave." Bam!

The Bible says that fear went throughout all the Church. You can be sure it did! And here is another apostle who points his finger at a false prophet — someone who is trying to pervert the Gospel — commands his eyes not to work, and they don't work!

An Evangelist With Discernment

Many years ago there was a healing evangelist who held tent meetings around the United States. A man plotting to write an article exposing the man of God walked up to the evangelist and said, "I'm blind." (He wanted to expose the evangelist to be a fraud.)

The man of God, discerning the intent of his question, asked him, *"What* are you?"

Again the man said, "I'm blind."

The evangelist said, "Would you say that again?"

"I'm blind."

The evangelist said, "So be it, according to your words."

The scoffer became blind, and the man of God walked away from him. Now that's discernment!

Fear would sweep the land if we started seeing some of those things happen. Or how about if some prophets would say, "God took me in the Spirit into your house, and I saw you beat your wife." You'd fall on your face and repent, or you'd probably be dead in a short period of time, if you didn't repent.

An Apostle-Prophet Missionary Team

We see more about apostles and prophets in Acts 15:

Then it pleased the apostles and elders, with the whole church, to send chosen men of their own company to Antioch with Paul and Barnabas, namely, Judas who was also named Barsabas, and Silas, leading men among the brethren.

Acts 15:22

These men were selected to carry a particular letter to establish doctrine in the Gentiles' churches.

Verse 32:

Now Judas and Silas, themselves being prophets also, exhorted the brethren with many words and strengthened them.

It says here that prophets should be exhorting and strengthening.

Verse 41:

And he went through Syria and Cilicia, strengthening the churches.

This refers to Paul, who "chose Silas and departed, being commended by the brethren to the grace of God" (v. 40). So before the Apostle Paul started his missionary trip to these regions to minister and strengthen the churches, he selected a prophet, Silas, to accompany him.

An Apostolic Squabble

Right before that, this great Apostle Paul and the great Apostle Barnabas got in a big agreement and it almost came to blows! It got to the point where the church members were almost choosing sides! The church was in danger of splitting.

Others had to come in and pull them back, as if they were athletes who had to be pulled apart at some sporting event. God was full of grace, because when they repented, He sent them back out to exhort the churches.

Prophets should *strengthen* churches, not tear them down. Prophets should build churches up.

Daughters Who Prophesied

On the next day we who were Paul's companions departed and came to Caesarea, and entered the house of Philip the evangelist, who was one of the seven, and stayed with him.

Now this man had four virgin daughters who prophesied.

Acts 21:8,9

Here we have four daughters who prophesy. Evidently there was a spirit of prophecy on Philip's house, because four daughters prophesied. That's a significant number. It doesn't say they were *prophetesses*. They could well have been, however.

Agabus the Prophet Warns Paul

The account continues in verses 10 and 11:

And as we stayed many days, a certain prophet named Agabus came down from Judea.

When he had come to us, he took Paul's belt, bound his own hands and feet, and said, "Thus says the Holy Spirit, 'So shall the Jews at Jerusalem bind the man who owns this belt, and deliver him into the hands of the Gentiles.'"

Remember, Agabus is the man who does illustrations as he prophesies. He went over to Paul, removed Paul's belt, got on the floor, wrapped the belt around his own feet and hands, and prophesied to "the man who owns this belt" (whom they all understood to be Paul). They also knew Paul was going to Jerusalem.

But here the prophet Agabus is correcting Paul; he is correcting an apostle! He says, "The man who owns this belt is going to be bound and handed over to the Gentiles."

Paul replies, "Well, I'm ready to go to jail and die for Jesus."

Paul Misses God!

Paul was so wrapped up in his own will that he was missing God. All along the way to Jerusalem, Jesus and the Holy Spirit sent prophets to Paul, and they prophesied words from the Holy Spirit that he not go to Jerusalem, but he still went.

The Jews did not wrap Paul up in chains and put him in prison. Instead, they convinced him to shave his head and take a vow. They actually convinced him to walk according to the Law when he had preached living by grace, not the Law!

Paul destroyed his testimony to the point that the Jews would not listen to him. A riot broke out, they turned him over to the Gentiles, and the prophecy came to pass. Agabus had given Paul a prophecy concerning going into imprisonment.

Prophets and Self-Control

Prophets are supposed to be spiritual people. Spiritual people should have self-control. I Corinthians 14:32,37 says:

And the spirits of the prophets are subject to the prophets.

If anyone thinks himself to be a prophet or spiritual, let him acknowledge that the things which I write to you are the commandments of the Lord.

Paul is giving instructions to prophets here. When he says that the spirit of the prophet is subject to the prophet, it means you can't get away with the excuse, "I just couldn't *control* myself; God *made* me to do it!" If you say this, you're losing yourself to technique, mannerisms, and approach. And you're breaking the structure of a decent, orderly service.

How many times have I heard people declare, "God made me do it. I didn't want to do it, but I had to, because God was telling me to do it."

You have to wonder, "Did God *really* tell them to do that?" For instance, when people do things that God supposedly told them to do, but then they find themselves in a financial crisis after they've done it, you really wonder! No wonder the world tends to look down on the Christians' lack of financial savvy.

Chapter 4
Four Categories of Prophets

Now let's examine the structure of the prophet. To begin with, there are four categories of prophets:
1. *Foundational prophecy*
2. *Prophetic gifting*
3. *Prophetic ministry*
4. *The office of prophet*

Foundational prophecy has the least amount of God's Word in its prophecy, and the most amount of man's word in it.

Prophetic gifting has more of God's Word involved, a little more accuracy, and a little more divine revelation than #1.

Prophetic ministry has even more of God's Word, is far more accurate, and includes more divine revelation than #2.

The office of prophet has the most Word, accuracy, and revelation in it.

Let's look at *foundational prophecy* in detail. Any believer can prophesy, according to scripture. For example, Acts 2:17 says,

> "... I will pour out My Spirit on all flesh; your sons and your daughters shall prophesy...."

A definition of *foundational prophecy* is: Any believer who speaks something God has brought to mind that results in the edification of the hearer (I Corinthians 14). Acts 2:17,18 tells us that it can happen to all believers.

Those who are operating on the first level, *foundational prophecy*, should not be speaking in church services, but could begin in small group meetings. They are not ready yet to move out in the congregation.

The majority of people who are speaking in congregations today are operating in level two, or *prophetic gifting*. There are far fewer operating in the third and fourth levels.

I Thessalonians 5:20,21 tells us, "Do not despise prophecies. Test all things; hold fast what is good." Thus, we shouldn't despise *foundational prophecy*, or any prophecy, but we should hold to what is good. This means we should judge all prophecy according to the Word of God, and we should hold onto the good part.

Desire To Prophesy!

I Corinthians 14:39 admonishes us, "Therefore, brethren, desire earnestly to prophesy, and do not forbid to speak with tongues." Every believer should desire to prophesy! This doesn't mean walking in the *office of prophet*; it means *foundational prophecy*, which is open to all believers.

I Corinthians 13:2 says, "And though I have the gift of prophecy, and understand all mysteries and all knowledge, and though I have all faith, so that I could remove mountains, but have not love, I am nothing."

This means that even before we desire to prophesy, we should be walking in the love of God. The love of God should prompt us to say, *"I want to be the best for my brothers and sisters in the Lord Jesus Christ."*

I Corinthians 14:1 tells us to "Pursue love, and desire spiritual gifts, but especially that you may prophesy." This refers to the whole Church; The whole Church should desire prophecy within its meetings. And it says in verse 39 that the individual believer should desire to prophesy.

To whom should the level one person prophesy the most? To himself. You should speak to yourself the words God gives to you. This is self-edification.

Since you are going to have *what you say*, you need to start *saying* what God wants you to *have!* Therefore, you need to start saying what God puts in your mind to have.

Foundational prophecy does not mean foretelling the future. Foundational prophecy is speaking something that God has brought to mind that results in edification.

Limits on Personal Prophecy

The person speaking under the category of *foundational prophecy* should never give personal prophecies to other people. Personal prophecy is defined as *telling someone his future, or telling someone God's will for his life.* For an example, someone may say, "God has shown me that you will have a husband a year from now."

That should never happen in level one prophecy. It is designed solely to edify, exhort, help, encourage, strengthen, and build people up. And the principal person who should be the recipient of such prophecy is *you*.

That's why Paul said, ". . . let him who speaks in a tongue pray that he may interpret" (I Corinthians 14:13). He also says that interpretation of tongues is equivalent to prophecy (I Corinthians 14:5).

Become Self-Edifying

Paul is telling us that we should pray in tongues over our life and give the interpretation, or speak *foundational prophecy* over our life to be edified and prepared for our day.

In other words, we should be self-edifying individuals! Instead of being "down" all the time, we should be able to edify ourselves.

"But I need someone to help me."

Then go into your prayer closet with God. Start worshiping Him. Start praising Him. And start giving prophetic utterance.

Foundational prophecy is an encouraging word about God being your strength, God helping you, God overcoming fear, and God saying, "I will never leave you or forsake you." *Foundational prophecy is prophesying over yourself!* It is speaking the Word of God over your life.

I Corinthians 13:9 says, "For we know in part and we prophesy in part." All prophecy is in part; especially that in level one, which has a lesser part.

A Christian prophesies by faith. Romans 12:6 says, ". . . let us prophesy in proportion to our faith," or according to our faith. Do you have faith? Then prophesy according to your faith.

This doesn't mean finding other people and giving them "words"; it means giving utterances to *yourself* through the Holy Spirit. Edify yourself. Worship God in a prophetic way, building yourself up in the Holy Spirit.

Acts 19:6 says, "And when Paul had laid hands on them, the Holy Spirit came upon them, and they spoke with tongues and prophesied."

Here we see people who are born again, but they are not filled with the Holy Spirit. They have never spoken in tongues. Paul lays his hands on them, prays for them, and they receive the baptism in the Holy Spirit. They speak in tongues and prophesy.

People say, "Oh, you can't do that! You have to be saved for many years to be able to *prophesy.*"

What were they prophesying? They were prophesying *foundational prophecy* — simple edification to God and themselves.

Prophetic Worship

But *foundational prophecy* can even be divine worship, or worship by the Spirit. What I mean by this is, when you are so moved by the Holy Spirit that words of thanks to God just flow from your spirit to Him. That's when you enter into prophetic worship. That's when the *new song* will come from the Lord.

> Pursue love, and desire spiritual gifts, but especially that you may prophesy.
>
> For he who speaks in a tongue does not speak to men but to God, for no one understands him; however, in the spirit he speaks mysteries.
>
> But he who prophesies speaks edification and exhortation and comfort to men.
>
> He who speaks in a tongue edifies himself, but he who prophesies edifies the church.
>
> I wish you all spoke with tongues, but even more that you prophesied....
>
> **I Corinthians 14:1-5**

That phrase "even more" in verse 5 means "rather," or "in a greater degree." So Paul was saying, "I would that you all spoke with tongues, but rather, literally — in a greater degree — to the point that you prophesy."

Paul says that if you will continue to speak in tongues, prophecy will come out. Divine worship, prophetic utterance, and divine edification will come out of your mouth!

There is a practice I have in my own personal life, where I pray in the Spirit and let God speak to me through my own mouth in prophetic utterance, *foundational prophecy*. It is edification; nothing weighty. God brings to my mind things that will help in my day and the situations I will be facing.

Hearing From God Every Day

I'm one of those fanatics for Jesus! I believe we should live a Spirit-filled life. I believe that if God has given me the Holy Spirit, I'm to pray in the Spirit; and God will speak to me, and I will hear Him.

I talk to God every day. Some people say, "Oh, I want to talk to God." God *is* talking to you; you just have to listen to Him.

The best way to hear God is to pray in tongues to the point where you prophesy and hear God speak. But we're not predicting things in this practice; we're edifying, encouraging, and strengthening ourselves, for it says in verse 3 of I Corinthians 14 that *foundational prophecy* should be edification, exhortation, and comfort. It's made up of those three elements.

Verse 31: "For you can all prophesy one by one, that all may learn and all may be encouraged."

Now look at verse 24: "But if all prophesy, and an unbeliever or an uninformed person comes in, he is convinced by all, he is judged by all."

Paul is referring to people who are going to get to the place of prophetic utterance coming forth. Their worship and praise is going to bring salvation into their midst: Unbelievers are going to become born again.

Characteristics of Foundational Prophecy

As we have seen, all believers should seek to operate in level one, or *foundational prophecy*. The function of level one prophecy is found in I Corinthians 14:3, which tells us that all *foundational prophecy* should strengthen, encourage, and comfort. If it's not doing one or all of those three things, it's not of God.

Prophetic words are given for *specific* situations and circumstances. They are supposed to encourage you in the situations and circumstances you face. They are supposed to have meaning and help you.

For example, when you're in a small group, you may say to someone, "You know, I just got an impression that God wants to encourage you and tell you that you're doing good, and He really loves you." That's a prophetic word, and it may come forth in a small group, such as a prayer circle.

Or the word may be something like this: "I have a witness that God is doing something special in your life. You just need to be strengthened and encouraged."

But the word should *not* be something like this: "Thus says the Lord God Almighty, God declares your bondage and shackles are going to be broken. They shall fall to the ground as you praise and worship Him in a greater and more powerful way. And you will never see those powers of darkness overtake you again."

Why don't you just say, "God wants to bless you. As we prayed, I felt like God is really doing something in your life." That's a good word. Just be normal — don't overdo it!

Again, these words uttered on level one should never be personal prophecies, telling someone's future or telling them what they should do.

Means of Revelation

Most often, the means of revelation for *foundational prophecy* are simple concepts, thoughts, or ideas that God brings to your mind. You don't experience an audible voice, a vision, a dream, or an angel whispering in your ear; it's just a thought from God. These may well include a word of knowledge for a specific situation.

In this area, as people start to exercise *foundational prophecy,* they may get over into *prophetic gifting,* for there will be an overlapping of these two levels of prophecy. People don't move from one level to the next without having some overlapping occur. In the next chapter we will discuss level two, "Prophetic Gifting."

Chapter 5
Prophetic Gifting

We need to understand all four categories of prophecy and prophets, for it will allow us to place people into categories for the purpose of application. It will allow us to understand our limitations. And when we recognize our limitations, we won't step out into false doctrine or error, and we won't hurt people.

Starting an exercise program would be a good example of "knowing your own limitations." When you begin weight-lifting, you need to know your limitations, so you usually go to someone with more experience than you, such as an instructor.

The instructor will be able to help you know whether or not you are ready for weight-lifting. He may tell you to forget weight-lifting and begin with stretching. He may say, "Let's begin with a few sit-ups and push-ups."

You may argue, "Oh, I want to start pressing 225 pounds right now." That could put you in the hospital with a bad back!

We have to know our limitations so we won't hurt ourselves. We need to find out where we are spiritually.

Level Two

The second level of prophecy is *prophetic gifting*, which is the gift you will most commonly see in the church.

Prophetic gifting is defined as believers who regularly receive impressions in their hearts, and possibly dreams, visions, or other types of revelations.

God deals with people in different ways. Some prophets will act the word out, and some will speak it out.

There was a time in my personal life when my wife and I were being attacked. It was destroying our lives. It happened right before we were to teach at a marriage seminar, and it was the biggest attack on our marriage we'd ever had in our lives! We couldn't even be civil to each other!

A person in our congregation had a vision of a large demon standing over our bedroom. Acting on this vision, I walked outside looking over our bedroom, and commanded that demon to leave in the Name of Jesus. The demonic attack broke, and we were free.

A person operating in the area of *prophetic gifting* won't always have dreams or visions. In fact, he may never have a dream, but he may have a vision, or vice versa. Another may never have either; only impressions.

In the church today, many people need to be operating in the area of *prophetic gifting*. They would be categorized as local church prophets.

A Note of Caution

Unfortunately, some people want to use titles to gain control. A major concern of mine is that people are going to look at prophets as being tremendously authoritative. They are not going to understand the different categories of prophecy. They will think that they should obey every word that comes out of a prophet's mouth.

My desire is to help you understand that the word "prophet" is not a scary word. It should be a common word in the New Testament church. There should be prophets in the New Testament church just like there are ushers or Sunday School teachers. Prophets are *for* the church today.

Dreams and Visions

Those who operate in level two, *prophetic gifting*, should have either dreams, visions, pictures, or words with some interpretation and specific application accompanying the revelation. A believer may have a visitation from God once in a lifetime, but it doesn't mean he is a prophet.

The Book of Acts tells us about Ananias, a man in Damascus who had a vision. Jesus told him to go to a street called Straight and find a man by the name of Saul in the house of Judas (Acts 9).

Even though Ananias had this vision, the Bible never says he was a prophet or prophesied. He was a man who simply obeyed God; a man who'd had an open vision with specific instructions.

The Function of Prophetic Gifting

What is the primary function of level two? Primarily, the prophet's function is found in I Corinthians 14:3, "But he who prophesies speaks edification and exhortation and comfort to men."

Prophetic gifting is still controlled by those three elements (edification, exhortation, comfort), and it will be used in a congregational setting. *Foundational prophecy*, on the other hand, will be used in a small group setting and on a one-to-one basis.

Prophetic gifting used in a congregational setting should strengthen, comfort, and encourage the church, although the prophet will also receive words of correction and direction to give to the church.

How Revelation Comes

How does revelation come? It comes by regularly receiving words, visions, pictures, or dreams.

Prophets may occasionally have an open vision in which the Lord speaks directly to them and they hear the audible voice of God. They also may have open visions in a church service, such as seeing the Shekinah glory of God come in the form of a cloud.

They will be used by the Holy Spirit in the gifts of healings, miracles, and so forth, because prophecy opens the door to other manifestations of the Spirit of God.

Guidelines for Prophets

Levels two, three, and four of prophecy fall under the guidelines of I Corinthians 14:29-31:

Let two or three prophets speak, and let the others judge.

But if anything is revealed to another who sits by, let the first keep silent.

For you can all prophesy one by one, that all may learn and all may be encouraged.

What is the best way for two or three prophets to speak so other prophets can judge? The best way would be if the *prophetic gifting* is getting some insight that is beyond simple inspirational prophecy.

There are two types of prophecy: one is inspirational, and the other is revelational.

Inspirational prophecy doesn't mean there should be judgment by the other prophets. If it's revelational prophecy, meaning, the foretelling of a future event, the direction of the congregation, or a corrective word, *it should be submitted in writing to the leadership of the church before it is given publicly.*

Therefore, two or three prophets can get together and speak the prophecy and the others can judge it to see if it is a correct word from the Lord. Then they can give it to the congregation. This way, the congregation will be protected against false prophecy.

Submitting Written Prophecies

When prophets get dreams and visions, or a prophetic word that has to do with correction or future events, they should write them down and submit them to the church leadership. The pastor should call in several prophets and ask if they have anything from the Lord along the same lines.

If they have, they should judge it to make sure the prophet is in line with God and then bring it forth to the congregation, so that all will be edified.

A few years ago, there were four attacks from the enemy on our congregation. A member of our congregation had a prophetic dream revealing this attack. The dream was written down and submitted to me.

I then took it to the Lord, prayed, and was able to judge it. I was tremendously impressed by the Holy Spirit that this dream was from God and so delivered it to the congregation. Through this dream, our congregation was corrected and delivered from these attacks before any damage was done.

Five Prophets Needed

Each church should have at least five people operating in *prophetic gifting*. According to verse 29, "Let two or three prophets speak, and let the others judge."

The word "others" is plural, which means at least two people are involved besides the "two or three prophets" which are mentioned first. Therefore, there should be at least five prophets in every congregation.

Those involved in the *prophetic gifting* are *lay people* who are in tune with God. They may be housewives, gas station attendants, businessmen, and so forth. They are people who work secular jobs. God has given them gifts. They must nurture and be good stewards of these gifts for Jesus Christ and the edification of the local church.

Chapter 6
Prophetic Ministry

The *prophetic ministry*, or level three, is made up of those who are in full-time ministry. Their gifting has been recognized, nurtured, and commissioned in the local church for regular ministry.

There are prophetic ministers in the land who are not prophets. Their characteristics include the facts that they are full-time ministers who have respect from their peers and from the congregation. They have the authority to correct, rebuke, and direct.

Note that the authority to rebuke does not extend to those operating in levels one or two.

Characteristics of a Prophetic Minister

A prophetic minister is mature in character, mature in spiritual matters, and mature in unity with God's corporate purpose. They are trying to bring the church together and make it stronger; not divide it. They are supportive of, and in unity with, the local church. They also operate in the prophetic gifts.

These gifts are found in I Corinthians 12. They include: healing, miracles, powers, prophecy, discerning of spirits, and faith.

If a person does not have signs and wonders happening, he is not in *prophetic ministry*. He could be an anointed teacher, preacher, or exhorter, however. There are people who are great exhorters who are proclaiming themselves to be prophets. They are not prophets; they are exhorters.

Paul did special signs and wonders. He also proclaimed that there are certain signs that apostles do, and he did those signs before the people. There are certain signs that apostles do that other ministries don't do.

The function of a *prophetic ministry* is to give direction and correction, and to fulfill other services in line with I Corinthians 14:3. This means they should be edifying, exhorting, and comforting.

They are to help illuminate and articulate the specific truths or doctrines the Lord is seeking to emphasize, because the *prophetic ministry* declares what the Holy Spirit has to say to the Church.

Receiving Revelations

How do people in *prophetic ministry*, level three of prophecy, receive revelation?

1. They frequently receive words, dreams, and visions.
2. They have dreams more frequently than people on the second level *(prophetic gifting)*. *Prophetic ministry* sees into the spirit world. In Acts 2:17, it states that in the last days God will pour out His Spirit on all flesh; our sons and daughters shall prophesy; our old men and young men shall have dreams and visions. These manifestations should be regular events in the *prophetic ministry*.
3. A prophetic minister can have open visions occasionally. They should regularly have words from God, including some dreams and visions.
4. Prophetic ministers should have words from God that are divinely inspired, spontaneous utterances that they have not given before. The Holy Spirit drops these utterances into their heart as they are speaking or preaching.

Chapter 7
Office of Prophet

The fourth level of prophecy is the *office of prophet*. A prophet is a believer who ministers in signs and wonders and has the greatest consistency in speaking words from God.

Prophets are extremely consistent and *accurate* in their words. They also operate regularly in signs and wonders. The characteristics of a prophet are:

1. They have been proven in years of ministry. They are *seasoned*. A person grows into the *office of prophet*. The number of years cannot be defined, but a prophet needs to have a proven track record.
2. Prophets have *suffered* for the Gospel. James 5:10 says, "My brethren, take the prophets, who spoke in the name of the Lord, as an example of suffering and patience."

Prophets are examples of suffering. A person pays a price to be a prophet. This doesn't mean that God will punish you if you are a prophet; it means that you will suffer persecution from the world. Also, those in the *office of prophet* at times will have to separate themselves to be with God and learn to know Him better.

The Greek word for "prophet" has two meanings to it:
1. To speak on behalf of
2. To speak before

This means the prophet should, first of all, speak *before* God and, second, speak *on behalf of* God. If the prophet never has an extended period of private time with God, he can never speak *before* God, so how can he speak later *on behalf of* God?

The suffering a prophet experiences stems from the price he pays to follow God in patience and do what God has called him to do.

Characteristics of Prophets

The prophet may be called to step out into areas where other people have not gone before. He must be extremely strong in faith, because God is going to send him to complete strangers to give them words, correction, edification, instruction, healing, and miracles. Those who stand in the *office of prophet* must be bold!

Their words carry much *authority* as they speak the Word of God more accurately than others. They also have more authority than those operating in the first three levels of prophecy.

Prophets will also frequently minister in *signs and wonders*.

The Prophet's Function

The function of a prophet is to provide *direction* and *correction* to those in church leadership. The prophet can have a word from God to tell the pastor about something happening in his church. This doesn't take the form of a general message; it is a specific, detailed word that he had no way of knowing except by the Spirit of God.

Prophets are to establish, articulate, and emphasize what the Spirit is saying to the Church.

I believe that those standing in the *office of prophet*, level four, are the ones referred to in Ephesians 4:11. Those operating in the first three levels are not included in Ephesians 4:11; they are found in Romans 12, I Corinthians 14, and I Corinthians 12.

The ministry gifts listed in Ephesians 4 are all anointed to articulate God's will for the Church; to direct, correct, and encourage the Body of Christ. All of them are anointed.

Prophets don't simply say, "God is going to bless your congregation"; they will be much more specific, perhaps even naming dates and events. They will foretell the future.

Revelations from the Holy Spirit

How do prophets get revelation from the Holy Spirit?
1. They receive an almost constant flow of divine revelation.
2. They have open visions. Some of these visions may be of the prophet being someplace else. They may even be translated to another location!
3. They may give both spiritual and secular predictions and information having to do with the world.

Prophets should have national and international recognition within their circle of influence. However, a person in the *office of prophet* will have only as much influence as people who recognize his office will give him. Nevertheless, the ministry of a prophet will touch other places, not just the local church, and there will be recognition for the prophet in those places.

As you know from the definition we gave, there are fewer people in the *office of prophet* than people operating in the other levels of prophecy.

Those who are operating in *prophetic gifting* (level two) are recognized in I Corinthians 14 as prophets — prophets in the local church. Did you know that prophets in the local church can be ushers, choir members, children's church teachers, and others?

All prophets prophesy according to their faith. They are limited by their doctrine, their faith, and their knowledge of God's Word.

Chapter 8
Administering the Prophetic Gifts

Let's look now at administering the prophetic gifts. How do we let people prophesy in the church, how do we administrate it, and how do we correct it?

I would like to make this statement: There are people who are going to declare themselves prophets. They will even have the signs of a prophet, and they will lift themselves above the office of pastor and demand that pastors submit to them and get direction from them. I believe that is absolutely wrong.

The *office of prophet* is in the Church. It went out from the Church. It says in I Corinthians 12:28:

> **And God has appointed these in the church: first apostles, second prophets, third teachers, after that miracles, then gifts of healings, helps, administrations, varieties of tongues.**

The words "first," "second," and "third" do not have to do with a line of authority; they have to do with chronological time. The apostle is not in authority over the pastor. *The prophet is not in authority over the pastor.*

In fact, when there was a dispute in Antioch about a certain doctrine, and what the Gentile Christians could eat and do, the apostles Paul, Barnabas, Silas, and others, along with the prophets, got together and said, "We must go to Jerusalem and submit ourselves to him (the pastor) and ask them what we should do." They sent a committee to Jerusalem. This committee, led by the Apostle Paul, went to Jerusalem to see James, who was the pastor of the church there.

They said, "James, here is the situation." Peter spoke (Acts 15), Paul spoke, and other people gave testimony. After James listened to all of them, he stood up and spoke by the Holy Spirit, giving the answer. And they all said, "We submit to you, James."

The Line of Authority

In that example, the Holy Spirit has given us the line of authority. God has set Jesus to be the Shepherd of the Church. He has set under-shepherds, who are pastors.

The pastor needs to be a person of prayer who can hear the voice of God. He submits himself to the Holy Spirit and to the leadership of the church in the sense of being open to visions, dreams, correction, and direction from apostles and prophets. But when it comes to a dispute, you sit down, pray, discuss, and submit to the pastor.

If you start telling prophets that they are the authority over five or six pastors, and all of these pastors need to check with the prophet for permission to act, you are wrong in doctrine.

God has set church government in the church, and when it is operating correctly, it will bless everyone.

The Pastor: Highest Authority

The pastor is at the highest position of authority in the New Testament Church, next to Jesus Christ. We submit to the pastor.

Who is the authority of the local family? The man. But does that mean that the man has the right to tell the woman everything she can and cannot do and dictate her life? No, it doesn't. It does mean that he is responsible for the direction that the family goes.

A pastor should never lord it over his congregation. He should never tell them, "You'd better listen to me. You can't do anything unless you do this and that." But when it comes down to making the final decision, that's the pastor's role.

You may think this is an enviable position, but when we get to heaven, guess who must stand in front of God and answer His question, "Did your church accomplish its mission?" The pastor can't use the excuse, "Oh, don't blame me. Blame the prophet who told me to do it." God may say, "I put you there. You are the one who must answer for it."

That's a big responsibility. The only way you can fulfill it is through humility and by being open to the Holy Spirit and what God wants to do in the church. So the *office of prophet* needs to be submissive to a pastor.

Guidelines for Prophecy

How do we administrate the gift of prophecy? What is church order? According to I Corinthians 14:40, "Let all things be done decently and in order." That is the guideline for the gifts.

There are three aspects to administrating prophecy:

1. Revelation
2. Interpretation
3. Application

The aspects of administrating revelation fall on the church leadership. The leadership can help those people who are beginning to move out in the gifts by fine-tuning their means of receiving revelation.

They can submit their questions to the pastor. They can ask, "I had a dream, and here's what it was. How do I handle it? What is it?" As you talk through it together, they learn the process of receiving *revelation* from God.

Interpretation needs to be received through the congregation, and it should be administered according to I Corinthians 14:8,9:

For if the trumpet makes an uncertain sound, who will prepare himself for battle?

So likewise you, unless you utter by the tongue words easy to understand, how will it be known what is spoken? For you will be speaking into the air.

What Paul is saying is, if you're going to prophesy or give an interpretation of a tongue, it needs to be easily understood. If you make it so complicated that people can't understand it, then all you have done is spoken into the air! Prophecy needs to be given to the people in a way they can *understand* it.

Application of prophecy falls into the category of judgment of prophecy. How you judge it is how you will apply it.

Personal Prophecy Examined, Limited

Before we get to the subject of judgment of prophecy, let us look at personal prophecy. Personal prophecy is when someone comes and delivers a specific word about your life, giving you direction, foretelling future events, or telling you what God's will is for you and what you should be doing.

Persons operating in level one, *foundational prophecy*, should never give personal prophecy. Those in level two, *prophetic gifting*, should give personal prophecy only in an exhortive way, submitting it to leadership or to the person who you think it is for. It should not be a rebuke; it should always be edifying.

Personal prophecy can be given on a one-to-one basis from someone not in leadership through a *trusted* relationship. That is after you have watched someone's life and he or she has proven their gift, their maturity, and their humility to the Holy Spirit. Then you know them and you can trust them.

Personal prophecies can begin to be delivered by those operating in level two, but they are more frequently delivered by those operating in the next two categories, *prophetic ministry* and the *office of prophet*.

Those in the third level, *prophetic ministry*, can give personal prophecies because they have the ability to direct, correct, and rebuke. And those in the fourth level, the *office of prophet*, will naturally give personal prophecies more frequently than the other three levels.

Is Personal Prophecy Scriptural?

The question is: Does God want people to have personal prophecies? Let's look for our answer at I Timothy 1:18,19:

This charge I commit to you, son Timothy, according to the prophecies previously made concerning you, that by them you may wage the good warfare,

having faith and a good conscience, which some having rejected, concerning the faith have suffered shipwreck.

Paul is saying that Timothy had received some personal prophecies which were designed to strengthen his faith. They were meant to give him confidence and a good conscience. He was to wage a good warfare through those personal prophecies, for they had given him the ability to do this.

So we find that Timothy, for one, has received personal prophecies. Someone has prophesied over him and given him direction, correction, and inspiration. So much detailed information was contained in these prophecies that Timothy was able to wage a good warfare.

Therefore, personal prophecy should help people wage a good warfare; it should help them have a good conscience; and it should result in their being encouraged, strengthened, and given direction.

Paul writes in I Timothy 4:14, "Do not neglect the gift that is in you, which was given to you by prophecy with the laying on of the hands of the presbytery."

Presbyters are in level three *(prophetic ministry)* of the prophetic ministries. These people had anointed Timothy for ministry, and they had laid hands on him. When they laid hands on him, they were able to discern what his calling was, and they prophesied that calling over him.

So those in level three can give personal prophecy to people. They can reveal the person's gift and calling.

Evidently, Timothy was given a word about his gift. Later on, he started to doubt his calling. "Maybe I am not to be a pastor," he thought. Paul told him to remember the prophecy.

There was Paul putting more weight on the prophecy given to Timothy than on the doubts Timothy had during this period of his life when he felt like he didn't know who he was or what was going on. He went through a time of confusion. Paul encouraged him with the words, "Remember the prophecies that were given to you."

Chapter 9
Judging Prophecy

One area we should be cautious about in prophecy is the foretelling of things to come!

Those operating in *foundational prophecy* (level one) should *never* foretell the future.

Those operating in *prophetic gifting* (level two) should *not* foretell the future.

Those operating in *prophetic ministry* (level three) may *sometimes* foretell the future.

And those in the *office of prophet* (level four) are the ones who frequently foretell the future.

Another area in which we should exercise caution is in guidance for a group or individual. If there is guidance for a whole group, such as directive prophecy, it should be submitted in writing to the leadership of the church, so it can be judged.

I believe that the majority of prophecy should come from the *prophetic ministry* (level three) as well as the *office of prophet* (level four).

A More Sure Word of Prophecy

Peter said, "We also have the prophetic word made more sure, which you do well to heed as a light that shines in a dark place, until the day dawns and the morning star rises in your hearts" (II Peter 1:19).

Peter is referring to the time he was on the Mount of Transfiguration with Jesus. Jesus had Moses and Elijah appear, and Peter saw Jesus in His glory. This was a prophetic, open vision — a prophetic visitation.

Peter saw the Son of God, Jesus, on that mountain. Jesus changed into His glory, Moses and Elijah appeared, and Peter knew by the Spirit who was Moses and who was Elijah. How did he know that? It had to be by the Holy Spirit, because he didn't know what they looked like.

When Peter writes in his epistle, "We have a more sure word of prophecy — we have something more sure than a prophetic vision or word," he is referring to the written Word of God. So when it comes to personal prophecy, if it does not agree with God's Word, put it "on the shelf."

There are realms of prophecy where we need to be cautious. For example, don't accept anything as absolute truth from someone you don't know, someone who isn't a prophet, or someone who can't give you detailed information. Just put their word on the shelf, and go on with your life.

Also, we should be cautious about the secrets of a man's heart being made known. The *prophetic ministry* does have an anointing from God to correct, direct, and rebuke, and thus the secrets of a man's heart can be revealed.

For example, once God gave me a word for a particular man in a service which revealed the secrets of his heart. I asked him during the delivery of this prophetic word if he was saved. Then I said he was involved in a business deal and he was trying to manipulate the situation. I gave him a warning from the Lord not to handle this deal in an evil way. The Holy Spirit revealed the secrets of his heart, and it resulted in his salvation, because the man came forward after the service and became born again.

Inspirational Prophecy

Now let's consider inspirational prophecy. You've seen a few vital points to use in distinguishing between *inspirational prophecy* and *revelational prophecy*.

Judging Prophecy

Many people — in fact, almost anyone — can give inspirational prophecy. That is in the category of level one of prophecy, *foundational prophecy*.

Inspirational prophecy is easy to give; especially during a time of worship and singing, when the move of the Holy Spirit becomes very evident. It can happen every time we come together — at every prayer meeting and every worship service — but there should be restraints on it.

When it is so regular, it loses its punch, or influence. Inspirational prophecy has a tendency to become "old hat," and we can become blasé about it.

Revelational Prophecy

On the other hand, revelational prophecy should be coming from the written submission of *prophetic gifting*, the spoken, spontaneous word of *prophetic ministry*, or the *office of prophet*.

Prophecy that has a more revelational quality would include elements of new direction, correction, doctrine, or practice that has been officially received by leadership.

This means that revelational prophecy goes beyond simple edification; it also includes some kind of direction or encouragement, strengthening, or a particular teaching.

If you give revelational prophecy and there seems to be a regular inaccuracy to it, you need to accept the fact that you do not have this gifting, and you should stop giving revelational prophecy. Pray that *other* people will have a word for your church.

Everyone should be encouraged to set aside any prophecy that doesn't immediately mean something, or witness to them. In other words, if you have to sit down and think, "Now, what does that mean?" just put it on the shelf. Don't reject it — remember it — but don't live by it. See if God will reveal it to you later on. This is the way we need to encourage people to handle revelational prophecy.

Hold Fast to the Good

I Thessalonians 5:19-22 tells us:

Do not quench the Spirit.

Do not despise prophecies.

Test all things; hold fast what is good.

Abstain from every form of evil.

When people prophesy, there will be some elements of good in it and some elements that may not be so good. Hold fast to that which is *good* in prophecy.

Paul writes in I Corinthians 13:9 that we know in part, and we prophesy in part. Since we only know in part and prophesy in part, we should be careful about not getting too long-winded when we begin to prophesy in the church!

Why? Because the longer a prophecy gets, the more doubts people have that it is of God; especially if it is inspirational prophecy. Inspirational prophecy should be on the short side rather than the long side. Hold to the good part.

How To Judge Prophecy

Paul says that all prophecy should be judged: "Let two or three prophets speak, and let the others judge" (I Corinthians 14:29).

In Matthew 7:15-20, Jesus said, speaking of true and false prophets, "You will know prophets by their fruit." What that means is, after they've blown in, blown up, and blown out, what's left?

What are the people they ministered to doing with their lives? Are their followers having their lives crumble before them? Are they getting weird? Wacky? Off-base? What is their fruit like?

Their fruit is not the car they drive. Their fruit is not the budget they have for their ministry. Their fruit is how the congregation is living after they're gone.

Are marriages changing? Are people being healed? Are people being turned on to Jesus? Are people getting more excited about God? Is the Word of God alive in them and affecting their lives? You'll know them by their fruit. All prophecy has to be judged.

Judged by the Written Word

For we did not follow cunningly devised fables when we made known to you the power and coming of our Lord Jesus Christ, but were eyewitnesses of His majesty.

For He received from God the Father honor and glory when such a voice came to Him from the Excellent Glory: "This is My beloved Son, in whom I am well pleased."

And we heard this voice which came from heaven when we were with Him on the holy mountain.

We also have the prophetic word made more sure, which you do well to heed as a light that shines in a dark place . . . .

II Peter 1:16-19

Peter is saying, "On the Mount of Transfiguration, when we saw Jesus in His glory, it was a wonderful experience, and we thank God the Father for it."

That which we have in the writings of Peter, Paul, John, and James is more sure, more powerful, and more authoritative than any prophecy that a prophet, *prophetic ministry*, *prophetic gifting*, or *foundational prophecy* can give.

The written Word of God will always supercede any spoken, prophetic word.

When I hear someone say proudly, "Well, you won't find *this* in the Bible; it's what God showed me," I run from them! They're headed in the wrong direction!

If your methods are right — if you're meditating and studying the Bible — you'll always end up with the right revelation eventually.

If your methods are wrong, you can end up with the right revelation for a while, but eventually you'll go off track. Run from people who are teaching things that are not in the Bible. They may preach some truth now, but eventually they will fall into false doctrine and hurt a lot of people.

We're all aware of certain churches where one man started out right, was called by God, but years down the road began teaching "revelations" that weren't actually in the Bible.

If we are going to be prophetic people, we should be willing to be judged by the written Word of God. John warns us:

> **Beloved, do not believe every spirit, but test the spirits, whether they are of God; because many false prophets have gone out into the world.**
>
> **I John 4:1**

Test the prophets by the Word. Make sure they're correct. They should be open to judgment. They should be willing to be judged.

Finally, let's make sure our hearts are open to receive general words from the Lord. As a pastor, I want the fullness of the Holy Spirit in my church.

Let's keep the following scriptures in mind as we judge prophets and prophecy:

> **If anyone thinks himself to be a prophet or spiritual, let him acknowledge that the things which I write to you are the commandments of the Lord.**
>
> **But if anyone is ignorant, let him be ignorant.**
>
> **Therefore, brethren, desire earnestly to prophesy, and do not forbid to speak with tongues.**
>
> **Let all things be done decently and in order.**
>
> **I Corinthians 14:37-40**

> **Do not despise prophecies.**
>
> **I Thessalonians 5:20**

Section 2
Gift of Prophecy

Chapter 10
Desire to Prophesy

See that no one renders evil for evil to anyone, but always pursue what is good both for yourselves and for all.

I Thessalonians 5:15

If we are to be a spiritually minded people, and if we are to have a Charismatic church, we must become concerned about other people, and greed must leave our lives.

The Bible says, "See that no one renders evil for evil . . . ." When someone does evil to you, don't return the evil, "but always pursue what is good both for yourselves and for all." The word "pursue" means "to follow after."

Have you ever played the childhood game "Simon Says"? When the person in front of you says, "Simon says, 'Touch your head,'" everyone touches their head, or "Simon says, 'Touch your foot,'" everyone obeys. You do what the person tells you to do as long as they say "Simon says" first.

For Christians, the Word of God becomes "God Says" in our lives. So "pursue" means "I am going to follow after God and do what He does."

I Corinthians 14:1 says, "Pursue love, and desire spiritual gifts . . . ." The Greek literally says "spiritual things." The word for "desire" means "to be zealous, open to it, excited about it, wanting the things to happen."

Instructions About Spiritual Gifts

I Corinthians 12 gives instructions to *the entire congregation,* and chapter 13 gives instructions to *the individual* (concerning the operation of spiritual gifts). Chapter 14 gives instructions to *the leader* of the congregation on order and protocol of the spiritual gifts so everything will be done "decently and in order."

We are all familiar with the first three verses of "The Love Chapter," chapter 13:

Though I speak with the tongues of men and of angels, but have not love, I have become as sounding brass or a clanging cymbal.

And though I have the gift of prophecy, and understand all mysteries and all knowledge, and though I have all faith, so that I could remove mountains, but have not love, I am nothing.

And though I bestow all my goods to feed the poor, and though I give my body to be burned, but have not love, it profits me nothing.

What I get bothered about is people who do not believe in tongues or in the moving of the Holy Spirit in today's Church. When they read these first three verses of chapter 13, they say, "We shouldn't seek after spiritual gifts. We should all desire love. We should all walk in love."

And I have heard people say, "I don't want the baptism of *tongues;* I want the baptism of *love."*

My friend, if you are waiting for God to hit you over the head and — whoosh — suddenly pour some supernatural ability to love everyone all over you, it's not going to happen! As soon as you think you've got it down pat — "I love everyone. Brother, I love you. Sister, I love you" — God will bring into your life someone who will challenge your great "love" and maturity.

Someone will pop up who puts your patience, your faith, your commitment, and your spiritual walk to the test, and you're going to find yourself wailing, "O God, I don't love this person!"

Pursue Love First

In chapter 14, God tells us what to do. He says, "Don't throw away spiritual things. Keep them. Desire spiritual gifts. Be zealous for them. Pursue after them." But you can't pursue the gifts until you're pursuing love. And this begins in I Corinthians 13:4:

> **Love suffers long and is kind; love does not envy; love does not parade itself; is not puffed up;**
>
> **does not behave rudely, does not seek its own, is not provoked, thinks no evil;**
>
> **does not rejoice in iniquity, but rejoices in the truth;**
>
> **bears all things, believes all things, hopes all things, endures all things.**
>
> **Love never fails.**
>
> I Corinthians 13:4-8

The word "love" is the Greek word *agape*. This word is translated in your *King James Bible* as "charity" and in the *New King James Bible* and most other modern translations as "love."

I personally prefer the word "charity." I think charity is an excellent translation, because in our English language today, we do not understand the true meaning of the word "love." It is too broad in meaning. We say things like, "I love peanut butter. I love pizza. I love Mexican food. I love red sports cars." We use the word "love" too loosely.

But when do we use the word "charity"? Only in an attitude of taking something that we have and giving it to someone who doesn't have as much. That's why I think the word "charity" is a good translation, for God is telling us to give ourselves to others, and not to expect them to pay us back.

If I want to do something good for someone, but I do it for them with an expectation of something in return, I have attached a string to my giving, and it is not charity. I've done it out of a motive that thinks, "Maybe she will pay me back."

But when I do things for someone out of charity, then I can expect God to return to my life what I have sown into their lives.

No Strings Attached

Charity has no strings attached.

We read in I Corinthians 13:4, "Love suffers long and is kind." The word for "suffers long" has to do with a sacrifice. *Charity is a sacrifice, and suffers long.*

I believe *The Amplified Bible* interprets these verses the best. This version reads:

> **Love endures long and is patient and kind; love never is envious nor boils over with jealousy; is not boastful or vainglorious, does not display itself haughtily.**
>
> **It is not conceited — arrogant and inflated with pride; it is not rude (unmannerly), and does not act unbecomingly. Love [God's love in us] does not insist on its own rights or its own way, for it is not self-seeking; it is not touchy or fretful or resentful; it takes no account of the evil done to it — pays no attention to a suffered wrong.**
>
> **It does not rejoice at injustice and unrighteousness, but rejoices when right and truth prevail.**
>
> **Love bears up under anything and everything that comes, is ever ready to believe the best of every person, its hopes are fadeless under all circumstances, and it endures everything [without weakening].**
>
> **Love never fails — never fades out or becomes obsolete or comes to an end . . . .**
>
> **I Corinthians 13:4-8** *The Amplified Bible*

Love is a sacrifice. It suffers long and is kind. The word for "kind" used here in verse 4 is "grace toward other people." Love has grace toward others. This means you cut them some slack. That's grace.

Charity does not envy. Quit desiring what other people have. Be content with what you have, and God will give you more.

Verse 4 says, "Love does not envy; love does not parade itself; is not puffed up." The word for "puffed up" means "hot air." So love isn't full of hot air. In other words, someone who has hot air tells other people how great they are. Instead of singing, "How great Thou art," they sing, "How great I am!" And this is not what love is.

Someone will ask, "All right, what should we do?"

We should have sacrificial love toward others, a love that is given to others with no expectation of payment in return.

Verse 5: "Does not behave rudely, does not seek its own, is not provoked, thinks no evil."

Love thinks no evil. The evil this is referring to is similar to the evil in Jeremiah, a desire to destroy an individual or groups of people with your conversation.

> **Then they said, "Come and let us devise plans against Jeremiah; for the law shall not perish from the priest, nor counsel from the wise, nor the word from the prophet. Come and let us attack him with the tongue, and let us not give heed to any of his words."**
>
> **Jeremiah 18:18**

Love "does not rejoice in iniquity, but rejoices in the truth." You are not to rejoice in someone else's fall into iniquity. Neither are you to rejoice in the doing of iniquity, but rejoice in the truth.

Love rejoices in truth. It rejoices in what is taking place in people's lives as truth, or when God's Word, prevails in their lives. We understand that the Bible says, "thy word is truth" (John 17:17).

"Bears all things . . . ." The word "bears" is a great Greek word, because it means you have found someone who needs help, *you have built a roof over them* to protect them, and your roof doesn't leak! This means you can be trusted with the secret things of a person's heart.

Can you be a friend that someone can come to and share with, and you won't tell other people their secrets? Do you have a roof over your friendships that doesn't leak?

". . . believes all things, hopes all things, endures all things." What this is saying is that love never fails. If I'm pursuing love, I'm pursuing God Himself, because the Bible says God *is* love. This is telling me that in my purest love, I am to act like God would act in any situation. This is a powerful truth.

God wants us to be kinder to our spouses, our children, our friends, our pastors, and others in the church and society in general. In other words, let's calm our lives down and follow after God.

When the Perfect One Comes

Love never fails. But whether there are prophecies, they will fail; whether there are tongues, they will cease; whether there is knowledge, it will vanish away.

For we know in part and we prophesy in part.

But when that which is perfect has come, then that which is in part will be done away.

When I was a child, I spoke as a child, I understood as a child, I thought as a child; but when I became a man, I put away childish things.

I Corinthians 13:8-11

In verse 8, we have three very important words: fail, case, and vanish.

The words "fail" and "vanish" are the same Greek word. It means to "slow down and come to a stop." Just as if you're driving in a car and you saw a red light up ahead, you would apply the brake, bringing your car to a stop.

The Greek word "cease" means to come to an abrupt stop. If you were driving a car and hit a brick wall, you would come to an abrupt stop.

In this verse, we are told that one day, prophecies and knowledge will slow down and then stop all together. But tongues will come to an abrupt stop.

Desire to Prophesy

Verses 9 and 10: "For we know in part and we prophesy in part. But when that which is perfect has come, then that which is in part will be done away."

This is talking about *our bodies!* Our bodies are not perfect. When this mortal puts on immortality, tongues will cease.

One day the Church is going to be instantly removed from the earth, and guess what leaves with the Church? Tongues! That's when tongues will come to an abrupt halt.

But there will be a group of people who will still be prophesying, because it is written in the Book of Revelation that God will send prophets in the last days. However, fewer and fewer people will be prophesying. We will return to the office of Old Testament prophet. In other words, prophecy will slow down and eventually come to a stop during the Tribulation.

The same will happen with knowledge. It will slow down and come to a stop, because one day we will be with the Lord and we will know as we are known. It says in verse 9, "For we know in part and we prophesy in part."

Verse 11 says, "I was a child and then I put away childish things." What Paul is saying is, "Quit being a child about the things of God and go after love."

Verse 12: "For now we see in a mirror, dimly, but then face to face. Now I know in part, but then I shall know just as I also am known." Verse 12 is saying that the perfect, in verse 10, isn't here until we see Jesus face to face.

Love Is Eternal

Verse 13: "And now abide faith, hope, love, these three; but the greatest of these is love." Why is love the greatest? Because love will never, ever go away.

The Bible tells us that one day faith will no longer be necessary, because you'll be in the presence of God.

Also, hope will leave someday, because what do you need hope for if you see it? You hope for it because you don't have it. When you have what you hoped for, you no longer hope for it.

But love will never, ever leave. We'll always be loving. We'll always be walking in the commandment of love. Paul addresses this in I Corinthians 14:1: "Pursue love . . . ."

Go after love; follow after love. Don't let go of it. Chase it. Hold onto it. Make love your pattern. Walk like love walks, and talk like love talks.

It amazes me when I meet people who want to pray for the sick, they want to see people fall under the power of God, they want to see cancer and sickness leave people's bodies — yet they treat their wife horribly.

"Oh, she's not spiritual enough for me," they complain. Or the wife will treat the husband horribly. "Oh, he's just not in the Spirit," she says. Did God give you that person? You'd better love them.

Love First, Then Gifts

The development of spiritual gifts will not happen without the development of a love walk.

God wants you to have love developing inside you. He wants you to be a sharing and grace person, kind to other people. In other words, He doesn't want to leave you as He found you.

God found me ugly and said, "Oh my, do we have work to do!" He got some angels, gave them several textbooks, and said, "Here's what you need to know for this guy. You will be busy. In fact, we're paying you time-and-a-half because you'll be so busy with him."

God started to deal with me about the raging temper that was inside me. God said, "I've got to take that out of you. I've got to calm you down. I've got to get you to the place where you're so calm, you can hear the voice of the Spirit."

Spiritual Interference

Anger, jealousy, and envy will keep you from hearing the voice of the Spirit. It's like having hands placed over your spiritual ears when you allow these things to enter your life.

You can't hear the voice of God clearly. You can't see what He wants you to do. You can't distinguish the direction God wants you to go.

I Peter 2:24 says: "Himself bore our sins in His own body on the tree, that we, having died to sins, might live for righteousness — by whose stripes you were healed."

Most of us know that verse, but let's back up to verse 21. Before you get to the healing part of your life, let's get to the verse 21 part of our life: "For to this you were called, because Christ also suffered for us, leaving us an example, that you should follow His steps."

Christ left us an example. The word "example" means you have a piece of paper that is commonly called a "master." Jesus is the Master paper. You are the tracing paper that is laid down on top of Jesus, and *you are to trace Jesus' picture in your life*, for He is our example of grace.

You are to trace "He gave His life up for the brethren." He loved. When He suffered, He didn't retaliate. When they spoke evil of Him, He didn't say anything back. That is our example.

That is what we're supposed to trace. That is what we're supposed to be doing in our lives: *We're supposed to be like Jesus!*

Chapter 11
Preparation to Prophesying

Pursue love, and desire spiritual gifts, but especially that you may prophesy.

For he who speaks in a tongue does not speak to men but to God, for no one understands him; however, in the spirit he speaks mysteries.

But he who prophesies speaks to men for edification, exhortation, and comfort.

He who speaks in a tongue edifies himself, but he who prophesies edifies the church.

I wish you all spoke with tongues, but even more that you prophesied; for he who prophesies is greater than he who speaks with tongues, unless he interprets, that the church may receive edification.

I Corinthians 14:1-5

I Corinthians 12 is written to *the congregation*. It addresses the congregation as a whole.

I Corinthians 13 zeroes in on you as *an individual* and what God wants you to do as an individual. We discussed in the last chapter about walking in love, what God wants us to do in love, and how God wants us to treat one another.

I Corinthians 14, on the other hand, zeroes in on the organization of a service, which means it addresses *the leaders* of the service, the ones who are responsible to answer to God for the order of the service. This chapter will be directed mostly to the pastor of the congregation.

We start with I Corinthians 14:1: "Pursue love, and desire spiritual gifts [things]," or to be spiritual. Your Bible may say "spiritual gifts." The word "gifts," however, is not in the original Greek. It means having a spiritual life, being one who is spiritual.

Thus, speaking in tongues is part of being spiritual. Prophesying is part of being spiritual. And having the manifestation of the Holy Spirit in your church is part of being spiritual.

A Word to Congregations

It is interesting to look at I Corinthians 12:31: "But earnestly desire the best gifts. And yet I show you a more excellent way."

The word "desire" is written in the second person plural. This is not addressing an individual; it is addressing a group of people; specifically the church at Corinth, and secondly all who read this letter.

Here it says in the second person plural, "But earnestly desire the best gifts." What Paul is saying is, "You *as a congregation* should be desiring that the best gifts are manifested in your congregation."

The word "gifts" is not referring simply to the nine manifestations of the Holy Spirit; it encompasses and includes the apostle, the prophet, the teacher, the working of miracles, the gifts of healings, speaking in tongues, helps, administrations, and so forth. Why? Because we found in previous verses that all these things are given to the Church so it might be edified.

The manifestations of the Holy Spirit were not in short supply at the church of Corinth. In fact, they had an abundance of prophecy, an abundance of tongues and interpretation — they had an abundance of the Holy Spirit manifesting Himself.

The Error at Corinth

Paul had to say to this church, "You come short in no gift or manifestation of the Holy Spirit (I Corinthians 1:7) — there's enough tongues, interpretations and prophecies going forth — but what you are not desiring is that the church as a whole be built up."

They were all seeking *individual* edification. They were all going after *self-recognition*; all were trying to be recognized.

As a congregation gets larger and larger, those who have a personality that needs to be the center of attention will start to yell louder because other people are being recognized.

If Jesus is the One who is being exalted, all of us are a part of the team exalting Him. Therefore, we're not going to seek self-edification or exaltation. Our goal is to see that the church is edified and built up, exalted in its community, and that we all work together as one unit, one family, and one body.

So in verse 31, Paul shifts from the congregation to the individual and says, "All of you should desire the best gifts." Continuing uninterrupted into chapter 13, he starts to teach on the best gift of all, love.

You know that Paul himself did not divide his letters into chapters; he just kept writing. He wrote, "And yet I show you a more excellent way," and then he said you should go after the love walk and make love your example.

"Pursue love and desire spiritual things," or be spiritual, he says in chapter 14, verse 1. Again, the phrases "pursue love" and "desire to be spiritual" are in the second person plural in the Greek. Paul is writing to the whole congregation.

Earnestly Desiring Prophecy

Paul is addressing all who count themselves as spiritual to follow after love and desire to be spiritual. It doesn't say that every individual should desire to prophesy, but that prophecy should be a manifestation in services of your church, and that all should desire that there be prophecy in the congregation.

We learn in I Corinthians 14 that Paul regards prophecy as the greatest gift. So if we were to address the question of which gift is the most important, Paul says prophecy is the most important. The second most important gift is tongues with interpretation, because tongues with interpretation is *equal* to prophecy.

In I Corinthians 12, the nine manifestations of the Holy Spirit are broken down in the Greek into sets of two, five, and two. Wisdom and knowledge are the first two. The next five are: faith, gifts of healings, the working of miracles, prophecy, and discerning of spirits. The last two are different kinds of tongues and interpretation of tongues.

Paul now enters into a teaching to pastors as to how they should teach their congregations about these last two manifestations, tongues and interpretation.

As we saw, Paul's statement in verse 1, "pursue love," is in the second person plural, and is addressed to all of us: "Pursue love, and desire spiritual gifts [things], but especially [desire] that you may prophesy."

When you pray, do you pray for the church, "God, I pray that prophecy will come forth. I don't have to be the one who prophesies, but I pray that prophecy would come forth?" If we're praying for prophecy, we're praying that the whole church will be edified and built up.

The Difference Between Tongues and Prophecy

Verse 2: "For he who speaks in a tongue does not speak to men but to God, for no one understands him; however, in the spirit he speaks mysteries." Note the word "mysteries."

Verse 3: "But he who prophesies speaks to men for edification, exhortation, and comfort" (to the church). Note the words "edification," "exhortation," and "comfort."

Verse 4: "He who speaks in a tongue edifies himself, but he who prophesies edifies the church." Again, note the word "edifies."

Verse 4 is a statement that is a spiritual law. Paul is stating this law to let you know it is true. There is something even greater to understand about this. In I Corinthians 14, although Paul is amplifying the greatness of prophecy, he is not demeaning or playing down the importance of the manifestation or the gift of speaking in tongues. He is not saying, "Let me tell you how unimportant tongues are," because they *are* extremely important.

In Paul's amplification of prophecy, we can understand how important tongues are, because Paul says, "He who speaks in a tongue edifies *himself*, but he who prophesies edifies *the church*."

That word "edify" is where we get our word "edifice." It means a superstructure, a building up, a causing to be made strong. This statement says that people who speak in tongues make themselves stronger. In what area? Would it be mental, physical, or spiritual? The answer is *spiritual,* because we're talking about spiritual things. But if you were stronger spiritually, wouldn't that affect your mental and physical life as well? Absolutely.

Making Yourself Spiritually Stronger

So Paul says, "If you pray in tongues, you build yourself up." You make yourself spiritually stronger. That means Christians should go about their business praying in tongues.

You should be driving your car praying in tongues (with your eyes open and hands on the wheel, of course). You can wash dishes praying in tongues. You can do lots of jobs praying in tongues. You can mow the lawn praying in tongues. You can pray softly in the Spirit almost anywhere.

When I first got filled with the Holy Spirit, people used to tell me, "You can't pray in tongues anytime you want to." But I'd already been doing it for months! I said, "What do you mean, you can't?"

"No, no, no. The Holy Spirit has to *come on you* and you have to have the Spirit *move* you. Then, when the Spirit moves you, you can pray in tongues."

I asked, "Then I can only get edified as the Spirit moves me. How will I know when I'm moved by the Spirit?"

"Well, you will know it because you can't sit still, and when it starts to come on you, you know you'd better pray in tongues."

That explanation still didn't satisfy me, because you only get those kinds of emotional experiences when you're in church. And Paul says that church is *not* the place where we should all stop and pray in tongues and nothing else.

We should not come together and spend an hour and a half to two hours just praying in tongues in a church service. If it's a prayer meeting, yes. If it's a time of intercession, yes. But not in a regular church service.

We edify ourselves when we pray in the Spirit, Paul says. What does this mean? The best way to explain it is to compare a 15-year-old child with a one-month-old baby. Both children have the same number of muscles. The 15-year-old wants to build his muscles up. He's not going to get new muscles; he just needs to build up the ones he has. So he starts to workout with weights, or he jogs, swims, or runs. What he is doing is developing what he has.

You have faith, and you need to develop it. You have spiritual muscles, and you need to develop them. You have the name of Jesus, and you need to develop it. You have healing, and you need to develop it. You have all things that pertain to life and godliness in Christ Jesus, but you need to develop them.

Praying in tongues is like lifting weights in the Spirit. When you pray in the Spirit, you are causing yourself to become stronger, lifted up, and built up.

It says here in verse 4 that the same benefit is received by the whole congregation when someone prophesies. In other words, when a prophecy is given, there is a building up of the church, a unifying, a bringing together.

Speaking Mysteries

Look again at verse 2: "For he who speaks in a tongue does not speak to men but to God, for no one understands him; however, *in the spirit he speaks mysteries.*"

When you pray in tongues, you are speaking *mysteries*. When you give a message in tongues in the congregation, however, it is still a mystery — and it will *remain* a mystery until someone gives the interpretation.

It is the interpretation that edifies. Tongues themselves do not edify. Nevertheless, the tongue edifies the individual who gives it. Why? Because that is the nature of the gift. The person giving the tongue is stepping out in faith, he is using faith, and he is built up.

Did you know that every time you speak in tongues, it's just as miraculous as raising the dead? Think about it! You are speaking a language you do not know — and you are speaking it perfectly — to God, and He understands every word!

Does the Devil Understand Tongues?

Many people have asked me, "Does the devil understand tongues?" My reply is, "What difference does it make? Is he bigger than God? Is he bigger than the name of Jesus?"

If I pray in my understanding in the name of Jesus, it's going to happen anyway. So if I pray in tongues, it's going to happen too. What difference does it make? It doesn't really matter. The devil can't stop my prayer, whether it's in English or in tongues.

I've had people tell me, "Don't pray in English. The devil will hear you and know your plans!" So what? It doesn't matter what he thinks, and I don't care if he knows what I'm going to do tomorrow. I'm still going to do it.

If I'm in the will of God, the devil's not going to stop it. But, do you know that? Of course, if I mess up, if I get in doubt, then I can stop it all by myself and this will give the devil place to come against my life.

The thing is, if I pray in the Spirit, I'm edified. If I pray in the understanding, according to the Word and the will of God, it's going to happen. I have this assurance according to I John 5:14,15. I have what I petitioned God for.

I have prayed out loud in English, "God, heal this person. God, heal my body," and it was heard by every spiritual being that wanted to hear it, and they never stopped it from happening.

Three Things Prophecy Does

Now look at verse 3: "But he who prophesies speaks *edification, exhortation* and *comfort.*" The word "edification" means "to build up." It is the same word that describes speaking in tongues: When you speak in tongues, you build yourself up.

I believe we should be people of tongues, because speaking in tongues is going to make us stronger. We need to be built up. We need that edification. Therefore, I believe we should go around praying in tongues as we perform our normal duties of life.

It says in verse 4 that when prophecy comes forth, there is a building up of the church. Therefore, prophecy does three things:

1. Prophecy should *edify.* It should build up. That tells me that if a prophecy tears down, points the finger, or comes against, it's not biblical prophecy for a congregation. There are offices that will point the finger, and they will do it in a way that will not tear you down. Correction should always build up and never tear down.

2. Prophecy should *exhort.* This word "exhortation" means "to come to one's aid, to be there when you need help, to give direction, to give encouragement, to give strengthening and then comfort."

3. Prophecy should *comfort.* It should calm and console. It means to comfort one by encouraging words.

Prophecy should be good for us!

Misguided Prophecies

Often people will prophesy something that God is personally dealing with them about. The Holy Spirit will come into their life and deal with them about it, and then they want to tell the whole world about it, excusing themselves from the message because they were the vessel that God used. They reason, "Since God used me, my lifestyle must be approved." That's a major mistake!

My point is that God is so loving, He's not going to have someone in the congregation who doesn't have authority recognized by the whole congregation to stand up, point his finger at everyone, and tell them how bad they are.

God doesn't want to point His finger and tell you how bad you are. He wants to point His finger and say what He's done for you so you won't need to stay that way. He wants to lift you up!

Don't look at a person and assume he's perfect just because great and mighty things happened, or miracles took place in his meetings. As soon as you start doing that, you're setting yourself up for a fall!

We need to constantly look at Jesus, who is the Author and the Finisher of our faith, who is the Apostle and the High Priest. We also need to be checking our lives. Paul said, "Examine yourself to see if you are in the faith" (II Corinthians 13:5). Look at yourself: Are you in the faith?

Right Motives for Prophecy

We need to have a right heart and right motives. Our motive should be that the whole church be edified, built up, blessed, and encouraged. When prophecy comes forth in the congregation, the people should be encouraged, exhorted, and comforted.

Those who prophesy should not tear people down; they should build people up.

When the Word is preached, people's hearts will be pierced. Their lives will be convicted, and the Holy Spirit will move on them to repent.

As an example, let's suppose God told you to stop drinking coffee. He didn't tell anyone else to do this; He just told you. Yet you get up and say, "Thus saith the Lord, coffee is horrible for you, and you'll never speak in tongues again if you drink it." That's *your* prophecy. That's *your* word from the Lord, not ours.

What God wants is to bring edification to the church and a coming together in unity, a bonding together, a growing together. Prophecy is the gift or door that opens up the four gifts that deliver people: miracles, healings, discerning of spirits, and faith. Prophecy leads to these gifts, because it says in I Corinthians 14:4, "He who speaks in a tongue edifies *himself*, but he who prophesies edifies *the church*." Paul continues in verse 5, "I would that ye all spake with tongues, but rather that ye prophesied" *(King James Version).* It's not a wish on Paul's part; it's a desire that's almost a commandment. The Greek word translated "rather" does not mean "instead of"; it means "so much that the result ends up in."

How Tongues Lead to Prophecy

So the verse is saying, "I would that all of you spoke in tongues so much that the end result is there is prophecy in the church." This tells me *the key to prophecy in the church is people praying in tongues!*

The way most prophecies come forth is when people start to pray in the Spirit. Prophecy is the gift that opens up the gifts that deliver people. And tongues and interpretation of tongues opens up prophecy in a greater realm than ever before.

The verse says, "I would that ye all spake with tongues" — literally, "so much to the point it resulted in prophesying."

Verse 5 concludes, "... for he who prophesies is greater than he who speaks with tongues, unless he interprets, that the church may receive edification."

Again, the whole reason we are seeking God is for the edification of the church — that the whole church is being edified, not an individual.

Why is the one prophesying greater than the one who speaks in tongues? Because the one who speaks in tongues will only bless one person — himself — whereas the one who prophesies will bless all who hear. So you can speak in tongues and have one person blessed, or you could bless 500 people through a prophecy.

The Next Move of God

Now let's look at I Corinthians 14:6: "But now, brethren, if I come to you speaking with tongues, what shall I profit you, unless I speak to you either by revelation, by knowledge, by prophesying, or by teaching?"

The word "revelation" means "to remove a cover." The word "knowledge" means "to know," or "knowing." The word "prophecy" means "to predict the future." And the word "teaching" is the word for "doctrine" — systematic teaching, stable teaching, line-upon-line teaching, doctrine.

Verse 6 begins, "But now, brethren, if . . . ." This word "if" means "If, and I do," or "If I come to you, and I do . . . ." Paul is saying, "If I come to you, if I happen to come to you, it's going to be by way of speaking in tongues." "If I come to you, and I do come to you speaking with tongues, what shall I profit you unless I speak to you."

Paul is saying, "I'm coming to you." Paul is traveling from city to city, and what is he doing *on the way* to that city? He's praying for that city. He's coming to the city speaking in tongues!

He says, "What good will it do you if I come to you, and I will do it, speaking in tongues? What will it profit you unless I speak to you by the four things: revelation, knowledge, prophesying, or teaching?"

What he is saying is, as I speak in tongues, I am speaking mysteries. I am building myself up. The four areas in which I build myself up are:

1. Revelation
2. Knowledge
3. Prophesying
4. Teaching

For instance, unless a pastor shows up in the pulpit and gives you at least one of those four areas, it will do you no good.

You would not be edified; you would get nothing out of the message. The pastor must deliver to you that which he was edified with through the speaking in tongues. He must give you what he received on behalf of you.

Now look at verse 21: "With men of other tongues and other lips I will speak to this people." Paul is saying, "I am sending ministers to you — pastors, preachers, apostles, prophets — and they are praying in tongues, and they are going to come and speak to you that which they have prayed, and some of you won't listen." That's what it means when he says, "With men of other tongues and other lips I will speak to this people; and yet, for all that, they will not hear Me."

"Tongues Are for a Sign"

Then it says in verse 22: "Therefore tongues are for a sign." Underline the word "sign." ". . . a sign, not to those who believe but to those who do not believe; but prophesying does not serve those who do not believe but those who believe."

Isn't it interesting that tongues are *a sign* not for believers, but *for unbelievers*? What are tongues for believers? They are *a means of edification*.

Therefore, tongues are a sign only to those who are unbelievers in the congregation, that they might hear another language, and that language might be interpreted — in a supernatural way.

Chapter 12
Guidelines for Prophecy and Tongues

A few years ago, some people tried to make themselves prophets. They went around prophesying to everyone, and they messed up many people's lives. I believe God has given me a message of warning to the Body of Christ concerning this.

There are two parts to this message:

1. Do not forbid prophesying.
2. Be careful not to build a ministry on just one gift, such as prophecy.

Anytime a ministry was built on one gift, it only lasted for a season and then fell. The Word of God is to be our primary means of guidance; we are not to look to prophets to be our primary source of guidance.

Prophets are simply to *confirm* what God is already doing or leading in our lives; they are not to *direct* our lives. The Word of God is the standard by which we live.

We must keep this in mind in the days ahead, for we will see people form prophecy groups. Error will arise in these "bless-me clubs."

Instead, I believe "prophecy clinics" need to be held where true men and women of God, full of the Holy Spirit and the Word, would teach congregations and leaders about what God is doing. This instruction would then remain within the churches, for I do not believe God has ever left the local church.

The only time God leaves a church and does something new is when the church says, "No, we don't want that." Anytime a church says, "God, we are open to what You want to do in our lives — go ahead and do it," He will continue to guide that church into full maturity.

Two Types of Prophecy

Something else to remember in these days when prophecy is a matter of great interest, is the fact that there are two types of prophecy.

There are two Greek words which are translated "prophecy." One type of prophecy is to *foretell*, to tell what is going to happen in future times, or to give knowledge of what is going to take place in the future.

The second type of prophecy is found in I Corinthians 14:3: "But he who prophesies speaks to men for edification, exhortation, and comfort." So this second type of prophecy is an *edification* prophecy, an *exhortative* prophecy, a *comfort* prophecy, a *confirmation* prophecy — a word that confirms, not foretells. It builds up, encourages, and strengthens the Body.

Type one is a *foretelling* of the future; type two is for *confirmation, edification, and exhortation.*

The Dangers of Personal Prophecy

I believe that the foretelling of an individual's future should come from the pulpit ministries, not from an individual in the congregation. Personal prophecy *can* come from Body ministry, but Body ministry should always be exhortative, comforting, and confirming, not foretelling.

A dangerous situation arises when people in the congregation go to other people and start giving such words as,

"God wants you to quit your business and get into this, or move from this place and go over to that place."

I believe that these specific, foretelling events should come from the proven ministries. Personal prophecy can come from Body ministry for edification and confirmation of *what God is already doing* in that person's life.

For example, if someone who was not recognized by the majority of a congregation as having leadership authority were to stand up in that congregation and prophesy something that was going to happen in the future that had nothing to do with plans that were publicly known, his message would not be widely accepted. The people would not accept him unless they had confidence in him. Such a person first needs to be recognized in his office or by the pulpit leadership.

Therefore, in the congregational setting, prophecy should always be edifying, exhorting, and comforting when it is addressed to the church, confirming what is going on, sharing that people are making the right decision and going in the right way. But *messages that foretell the future should come from recognized leaders in the church or the office of prophet.*

I have been in the ministry for more than 12 years, and in that time, few words from the congregation that foretold the future ever came to pass. On the other hand, when guest ministers came (who were consequently recognized with authority by the leadership) and gave words that foretold the future, almost all of them have come to pass.

Imperfect Vessels

What we must do is pray through, discover, and recognize the people in the church who are prophets and then give place to that gift and allow God to minister in prophecy through them. Even after we have done this, we must remember that when a person gives words from the Lord and foretells people's futures, it doesn't make them perfect; it simply means they have a gift!

I Corinthians 14:5 says, "I wish you all spoke with tongues, but even more that you prophesied...." The literal Greek says, "I would you all spoke with tongues to the point that you prophesied."

If you pray in the Spirit enough, you're going to get to the place of being able to prophesy: to be used by God to help other people, and to be an encouragement. Isn't that wonderful?

Jesus put it this way: "Out of your belly shall flow rivers of living water" (John 7:38). "Living waters" means you could be sharing with someone and be impressed by God to give them a Bible verse and read it to them. That's also prophesying. It's edifying. It's encouraging.

God will take people who step out like this, and He will mature and develop some of them into prophets and prophetesses. But they've got to start somewhere. So we should be praying in tongues to the point that it turns into prophecy.

I Corinthians 14:7-9 says, "And even things without life, whether flute or harp, when they make a sound, unless they make a distinction in the sounds, how will it be known what is piped or played? For if the trumpet makes an uncertain sound, who will prepare himself for battle? So likewise you...."

Paul is referring to us. He is calling those that prophesy a flute, a harp, or a trumpet! They are instruments of God.

Instructions for Prophets

Verse 9 continues, "... unless you utter by the tongue words easy to understand, how will it be known what is spoken? For you will be speaking into the air."

In other words, when you are giving an interpretation of tongues or a prophecy, it needs to be easy to understand. It also needs to be loud enough to be heard. It does no good if you give a word from the Lord so quietly that no one on the other side of the room can hear. No one will be edified then, for they have to *hear* it to be edified. And it must be easy to understand. Avoid deep, spiritual phrases that only a few understand.

Now let's look at verses 10 and 11: "There are, it may be, so many kinds of languages in the world, and none of them is without significance. Therefore, if I do not know the meaning of the language, I shall be a foreigner to him who speaks, and he who speaks will be a foreigner to me."

In other words, I can't communicate with an individual if I don't speak in a way that can be easily understood. If I go to people and tell them stories and pictures all the time, they won't know what I'm talking about, and they'll walk away, saying, "I don't know what he said; I can't understand a word he's talking about." *Make it easy to understand.*

The Correct Motive

Verse 12: "Even so you, since you are zealous for spiritual gifts, seek that you may excel for the edifying of the church." *Your motive should be that others can be blessed.*

Verses 13-15: "Therefore let him who speaks in a tongue pray that he may interpret. For if I pray in a tongue, my spirit prays, but my understanding is unfruitful. What is the result then? I will pray with the spirit, and I will also pray with the understanding. I will sing with the spirit, and I will also sing with the understanding."

This tells me that *all my prayers should not be in tongues!* It tells me I should pray in the Spirit, and I should pray in English. I should pray in English, and then I should pray in the Spirit. I should be using both.

Paul says in verse 16, "Otherwise, if you bless with the spirit, how will he who occupies the place of the uninformed say 'Amen' at your giving of thanks, since he does not understand what you say."

Sometimes we have a burst of praise to God. We lift our hands and shout and praise. And sometimes we do it in tongues. We should also do it in English so that those who are not familiar with speaking in tongues, or do not speak in tongues to give thanks to God, can say "Amen" at our giving of thanks.

Verses 17 and 18: "For you indeed give thanks well, but the other is not edified. I thank my God I speak with tongues more than you all."

In the Greek, "you all" means "all of you" collectively. Paul was talking to a church that was fanatical about speaking in tongues. The church had between 20,000 and 30,000 members, and he said to them, "I speak in tongues more than all of you put together!"

Speaking With the Understanding

Verse 19: "yet in the church I would rather speak five words with my understanding, *that I may teach others* also, than ten thousand words in a tongue."

Now we are moving into the office of the teacher. Verses 19 through 25 speak about teaching; they are for the benefit of the teacher.

It's better to speak five words that people can understand. It's better to say, "God loves you, and He is going to help you" than to stand up and give ten thousand words in tongues. That won't help anyone.

Verse 20: "Brethren, do not be children in understanding; however, in malice be babes . . . ." When it comes to anger, be as quick to forgive as little children are. Yet in the church we find adults who will get mad and not speak to each other for months! So we need to be like babes when it comes to anger or malice.

". . . but in understanding be mature. In the law it is written: 'With men of other tongues and other lips I will speak to this people; and yet, for all that, they will not hear Me,' says the Lord" (verses 20 and 21).

This is referring back to verse 6: Ministers are sent to you by God to teach you the Word "by revelation, by knowledge, by prophesying, or by teaching."

Verse 22: "Therefore *tongues are for a sign,* not to those who believe but to those who do not believe; but prophesying does not serve those who do not believe but those who believe."

The main theme of verse 22 is "a sign." Tongues are "a sign" to those who *do not believe.* If someone stands in a service and speaks in tongues and someone else gives an interpretation, it is "a sign" for the unbeliever.

On the other hand, prophecy is "a sign" for *believers.* The exercise of both gifts should have the same result — people being more open to God.

Verse 23: "Therefore if the whole church comes together in one place, and all speak with tongues, and there come in those who are uninformed or unbelievers, will they not say that you are mad?"

It is right here where most churches today are making a mistake. The whole local church assembles together in one place on Sunday morning, correct? It says here, "If all speak with tongues." However, most people who read this verse think it says, "If *all* of us, *all at once,* started to speak in tongues, people would think we were crazy."

Now look at verse 24: "But if *all* prophesy, and there comes in one who does not believe, or one uninformed, he is convinced by all, he is judged by all."

Does that mean that if all of us, all at once, began to prophesy and there was an unbeliever present, he wouldn't think we were nuts? Obviously, that is not what this is referring to.

The word "all" does not mean all those in the church. The key word is found in verse 19: "that I may teach." Paul is referring to all who are teachers; all who are about to teach at every service.

What it means is, if your teachers come up, one after another, and all they do is speak in tongues, someone listening will think they're mad. But if your teachers come up and *prophesy* — edifying the church, encouraging the church, building the church up — their hearts will be exposed and they will fall on their face.

This passage is not referring to the people in the congregation. I can't believe that if all in the congregation stood up and prophesied for five minutes, that would cause someone to get saved. It would cause some people to run out of the building! They would think everyone there was nuts.

Let's look again at verse 23: "Therefore if the whole church comes together in one place, and all (this is referring to all the teachers) speak with tongues, and there come in those who are uninformed or unbelievers, will they not say that you are mad?" Certainly they would.

Let's picture this scenario: The choir finishes singing. They sit down. The pastor says, "Open your Bibles." You open your Bible, and the pastor speaks in tongues for 30 minutes. Would you say, "Oh, that was a good sermon"? No, you would think he was crazy. Thirty minutes of tongues wouldn't help anyone.

Verse 25: "And thus the secrets of his heart are revealed; and so, falling down on his face, he will worship God and report that God is truly among you."

You see, when the person in the pulpit can point to people and say thus-and-so about their heart, those people are going to hear from the Lord.

Have you ever been in a service when the sermon you heard seemed like it told your life's story? You wondered, "Hey, was that pastor in my living room last night?"

What happened to you? *The secrets of your heart were exposed*, and you fell on your face. You were hearing from God in that situation, and it caused you to grow in Christ. This is how prophecy is to affect the church.

Let All Things Edify the Church

Verse 26: "How is it then, brethren? When you come together, each one of you has a psalm, has a teaching (referring to the teacher still), has a tongue, has a revelation, has an interpretation. Let all things be done for edification." That's the key: We should *edify* the church.

Verses 27 and 28 give us some guidelines on what should happen with everyone in the congregation; not just the teachers: "If anyone speaks in a tongue, let there be two or at the most three, each in turn, and let one interpret. But if there is no interpreter, let him keep silent in church, and let him speak to himself and to God."

Even though this is very simple, people can't seem to understand it. They make a mess out of it. It says that if there is a message or utterance in tongues, let it be two or three at the most.

The emphasis in the Greek is not on the *tongue*, but on the *person*. For example, let's say someone on one side of the church speaks in tongues. What the Bible says is, "Let that person speak in turn, two or three at the most, in turn, and let one interpret."

Guidelines for Tongues

When he or she is done speaking in tongues, there should be only one interpretation to that tongue. Someone else can give the interpretation, or that person can, but there should be *only one* interpretation. If two people feel moved by God (which often happens), whoever speaks first should finish it and the other should hold his peace.

So one person gives the tongue, and that person or someone else gives the interpretation. If a third person thinks to himself, "That interpretation wasn't right," he should keep quiet. Don't give an interpretation after that.

Another thing that happens is, the person who gives a tongue will also think he knows the interpretation. Then when a second person gives the interpretation, the first person (who gave the tongue) thinks that wasn't what it was supposed to be, so he decides, "I'm going to speak in tongues again because that wasn't the interpretation I wanted to hear." No, don't, because the Bible says you shouldn't. That is not for the edification of the church; that would be to get your own private message across.

Again, the emphasis is on *the number of people* who are going to speak forth messages in tongues in one particular service, *not* how many messages in *tongues* there shall be.

For example, when a person speaks in tongues, he is "marked" for that service. When someone else speaks in tongues later on, he is marked. Then, if there is a third person, he is also marked. No one else should speak forth a message in tongues, even if he should get one, because Paul is saying that the guideline is, there should only be *three* persons who give tongues.

Paul is giving this as a guideline, for it is just that, a guideline, not a hard-and-fast rule.

So, if three persons have now spoken in tongues and the interpretation has come forth, if there is to be another utterance in tongues, it should come from one of these three people. You can have five, six, or eight utterances, but they should come from no more than three separate individuals.

Why? Because if everyone is giving messages, people will think you are crazy. When God anoints these people, it keeps confusion out of the service and keeps things in order.

When To Keep Silent

"If there is no interpreter, let him keep silent in church," verse 28 says. You ask, "Well, pastor, how do I know if there's no interpreter?" By speaking in tongues and seeing if anyone gives the interpretation! It doesn't mean that someone who has the gift is not present; it means that God didn't give the interpretation.

So if you speak in tongues and we wait and wait and wait, and no interpretation comes, that is a clear sign to the rest of the church that no one else should speak in tongues. Everyone is to keep silent on tongues. If you do receive a tongue, you are to speak to yourself and to God. That's how you can know there is to be no interpretation in the service.

Verses 29 and 30: "Let two or three prophets speak, and let the others judge. If anything is revealed to another who sits by, let the first keep silent."

Preventing Arguments in Prophecy

Now we have two kinds of people who are supposed to keep quiet:

1. People who speak in tongues with no interpretation (they are to keep quiet for the rest of the service).

2. If you prophesy and then something is revealed to another who is present, the Bible says, "Let the first keep silent" or, literally, "hold his peace if something is revealed."

In other words, what God doesn't want to have happen is two people prophesying in an argument — one person prophesying his opinion and a second person deciding to prophesy a conflicting opinion.

All of us are to judge what is prophesied by the Word of God. The individuals themselves are also judged by the leader of the congregation and the other *recognized prophets*.

God commended the Bereans because they went back after they heard Paul and looked up the scriptures to see if what Paul was saying was true. Yet we have people today who hear a prophecy and say, "That's it! He prophesied!" And the catch-all excuse is when so-called prophets say, "The Lord said." They use this statement to give their words more weight.

However, just because someone says, "The Lord says," doesn't necessarily mean the Lord said it! People go around saying, "God said, God said, God said," and God's up in heaven saying, "I did? That's the first I've heard of it!" We need to be careful when we claim that "God said" something!

Verse 31: "For you can all prophesy one by one, that all may learn and all may be encouraged." Who's the "all"? All the prophets? This verse also refers to the congregation. *Foundational prophecy* is simple edification and building up. It is the ministry that *all saints* are called to do.

Prophecy: A Choice

Verse 32: "And the spirits of the prophets are subject to the prophets." You can't say, "God made me say it, and I can't help it. You've got to stop, pastor. I've got a word from the Lord." No, you need to sit down and be quiet, because you are subject to your own spirit. You can choose to yield to God and His order, or not.

Verse 33: "For God is not the author of confusion but of peace, as in all the churches of the saints." Thus, in every church the things that should rule our actions are:

1. order
2. decency
3. edification

Verses 34-36: "Let your women keep silent in the churches, for they are not permitted to speak; but they are to be submissive, as the law also says. And if they want to learn something, let them ask their own husbands at home; for it is shameful for women to speak in church. Or did the word of God come from you? Or did it only come to you?"

Paul's Word to Wives

There is only one word that is translated "women" in the Greek. It can be translated "wives" or "women." The context of the verse has to tell you which it is. Since Paul uses the word "husbands" in verse 35, we know the verse is referring to one classification of women, the married ones.

The word for "silent" means "to hold one's peace" or, literally, "to hold your own opinion." It's referring to wives: Let your wives *keep their opinion to themselves* while they're among other people in the church. In other words, the wives of the church leaders should not gather together in little circles at church and spread their opinions.

Literally, it says, "Let them hold their own opinion in the churches where they are not permitted to speak; but they are to be submissive, as the law also says." This means there was a group of wives who were neither submissive to their

Guidelines for Prophecy and Tongues

husbands nor to the church. They had opinions about how things were supposed to happen in the church. They were spreading their opinions among other people, and it caused strife.

Paul says that if they wanted to learn something, and if they really thought they were going around asking questions for their own knowledge, they should ask their own husbands at home. In other words, when the board meeting was over, he could go home and tell her what was going on. She could find it out that way, like everyone else, instead of sending her husband out on a mission to spread her opinions.

Verse 35: "And if they want to learn something, let them ask their own husbands at home; for it is shameful for women to speak" or, literally, "to spread their opinions or their decisions in the church."

These women were causing problems, and verse 36 is talking to them: "Or did the word of God come originally from you? Or was it you only that it reached?"

In other words, these women believed that they were the ones who knew what was right, and no one else did. This sometimes happens with men, too.

Verse 37: "If anyone thinks himself to be a prophet or spiritual, let him acknowledge that the things which I write to you are the commandments of the Lord." That seals it. If you are going to be spiritual, you'd better believe what Paul just said in this chapter.

Verse 38: "But if anyone is ignorant, let him be ignorant." If anyone wants to say, "No, I don't think only three people can speak in tongues; we'll have as many as we want," fine. Be ignorant!

Verse 39: "Therefore, brethren, earnestly desire to prophesy, and do not forbid to speak with tongues. Let all things be done decently and in order."

"Do not forbid to speak with tongues . . . ."

"Let all things be done decently and in order . . . ." That's the key to how the church is to operate: decently and in order.

Chapter 13
Questions About Prophecy

Here are some commonly asked questions about prophecy and prophets:

1. Is prophecy a perfect gift?

No. See I Corinthians 13:9,10 and I Thessalonians 5:20,21. The Bible tells us to judge prophecy. If it was perfect, it would not need to be judged.

2. Some prophecies we hear in church are full of condemnation for the whole church. Are these from God?

No. I Corinthians 14:3 tells us that prophecy is for edification, exhortation, and comfort.

3. Is all prophecy by Spirit-filled Christians inspired by the Holy Spirit?

No. The spirit of the prophet is subject to the prophet. People can give a word that they want to out of their own *head*. People can give prophecy out of their own *need*. I don't think we should prophesy except with a pure heart, for it's dangerous to abuse prophecy.

4. Can prophetic revelation be higher than the Word of God?

No. II Peter 1 tells us that the Word of God is a more sure word. The Spirit and the Word should always agree. If someone prophesies something that cannot be validated through the scripture, we do not accept that prophesy. It is judged to be incorrect.

There was once a church in Southern California where a woman stood up and started to prophesy condemnation. She said things like, "You are all sinners, you are no good, judgment is coming, God is going to make you sick," and so forth.

The pastor started to stand up to stop her, but the Holy Spirit said, "No, don't. Just sit down and watch."

The woman continued to prophesy things that did not agree with the Bible, and the congregation started to say in unison, "No! No! No! No!" They rejected it on their own.

The Holy Spirit told the pastor, "See? They will not accept it; therefore, it will not fulfill itself." Her "prophecy" was rejected by the entire congregation!

5. If I have an important decision to make, should I base my decision on the prophetic word of one person?

No. The Bible says, "By the mouth of two or three witnesses every word shall be established" (II Corinthians 13:1). You should never, ever make an important decision off the prophetic word of one person. It should always be by two or three witnesses.

And one of the witnesses should be the Holy Spirit inside of you, directing and guiding you in your own prophetic word that God tells you in your prayer time.

Prophecy is used to confirm something that has already begun inside of you. Prophecy is *not* to bring something new to you.

For example, a young single girl in my church was once friends with a certain young man, and the man prophesied over her that they were to be married.

She made a premarital counseling appointment with me and told me they were going to get married. As I talked to her, I asked, "Do you love this man?"

She said, "No."

Questions About Prophecy

"Then why are you marrying him?"

"Because he had that word from the Lord."

I had to explain to her how to judge personal prophecy. Thank God, they did not get married.

Prophecy doesn't start something new; it *confirms* something already present. The only reason this young woman was going to get married was because she thought God said she had to!

In Acts 13:2 we read an account about a group of prophets who met. The Holy Spirit said to them, "Now separate to Me Barnabas and Saul for the work to which I have called them."

Notice He used the word "called," which is *past tense*. They already knew they were going to be apostles. The prophecy confirmed what they already knew.